an ATTITUDE of GRATITUDE

ALSO BY KEITH D. HARRELL

• • • • • • • • • • • • • • • • • •

Attitude Is Everything: 10 Life-Changing Steps to
Turning Attitude into Action

The Attitude Is Everything Workbook: Strategies and Tools for
Developing Personal and Professional Success

▲ ▲ ▲

LOOK FOR THESE FUTURE TITLES

Attitude Is Everything™ Cards

Attitude Is Everything for Success:
Say It, Believe It, Receive It

The Attitude for Leadership: Taking the Lead and Keeping It

▲ ▲ ▲   ▲ ▲ ▲

All of the above are available at your local bookstore, or may
be ordered by visiting these Hay House Websites:
USA: **www.hayhouse.com**; Australia: **www.hayhouse.com.au**;
or U.K.: **www.hayhouse.co.uk**

an ATTITUDE of GRATITUDE

21 LIFE LESSONS

Keith D. Harrell

Hay House, Inc.
Carlsbad, California • Sydney, Australia • London, U.K.
Canada • Hong Kong

Published and distributed in the United States by: Hay House, Inc., P.O. Box 5100, Carlsbad, CA 92018-5100 • *Phone:* (760) 431-7695 or (800) 654-5126 • *Fax:* (760) 431-6948 or (800) 650-5115 • www.hayhouse.com • *Published and distributed in Australia by:* Hay House Australia Ltd., 18/36 Ralph St., Alexandria NSW 2015 • *Phone:* 612-9669-4299 • *Fax:* 612-9669-4144 • www.hayhouse.com.au • *Published and Distributed in the United Kingdom by:* Hay House UK, Ltd. • Unit 202, Canalot Studios • 222 Kensal Rd., London W10 5BN • *Phone:* 44-20- 8962-1230 • *Fax:* 44-20-8962-1239 • www.hayhouse.co.uk • *Distributed in Canada by:* Raincoast • 9050 Shaughnessy St., Vancouver, B.C. V6P 6E5 • *Phone:* (604) 323-7100 • *Fax:* (604) 323-2600

Editorial supervision: Jill Kramer   *Design:* Jenny Richards

Library of Congress Cataloging-in-Publication Data

Harrell, Keith D.
   An attitude of gratitude / Keith D. Harrell.
      p. cm.
   ISBN 1-40190-199-9 (hardcover) • 1-40190-200-6 (tradepaper)
   1. Gratitude. I. Title.
   BJ1533.G8 H37 2003
   179'.9—dc21   2002013480

Hardcover ISBN 1-4019-0199-9
Tradepaper ISBN 1-4019-0200-6

06 05 04 03   4 3 2 1
1st printing, August 2003

Printed in Canada

*This book is dedicated to my spiritual parents,
especially Dr. Creflo A. Dollar and Taffi L. Dollar,
who teach the Word of God with simplicity
and understanding. I thank God daily for
allowing me to be a World Changer—to make
a mark that cannot be erased.*

▼ ▼ ▼

CONTENTS

• • • • • • • • • • • •

A FEW WORDS
FROM THE AUTHOR

*"Life is a succession of lessons which
must be lived to be understood."*
— Ralph Waldo Emerson

As a life coach and teacher, it's second nature for me to view my personal story as ongoing lessons in living. Therefore, each chapter in the book ends with a life lesson—a point that I share with you to illustrate how obstacles can become opportunities for growth and transformation. My earnest hope is that by reading my story, you'll begin to reflect on and analyze your experiences . . . and in the process, look for the lessons in your own life.

ACKNOWLEDGMENTS

I owe my gratitude to all the wonderful people who made this book possible:

To Jan Miller and Shannon Miser-Marven, literary agents par excellence; to the wonderful staff at Hay House—Reid Tracy, Danny Levin, and editors Jill Kramer, Shannon Littrell, and Katie Tomkins—and to Bill Butterworth for convincing me I had a story to tell and for pulling it out of me—without you this book wouldn't have been written.

To my friend Arabella Grayson, whose candor and insight help me see and acknowledge difficult truths, thank you.

To my outspoken and loving sister, Toni Malliet, for a memory that never fails and for always being there when I need you most.

To my assistant, Donna Cash, whose hardy laughter, patience, friendship, hard work, and whatever-it-takes attitude allows me to get the job done—you're the best.

To Sara Kahan and Lisa Daniel for proofreading and polishing the final manuscript.

To Carolyn Zatto and Deborah Johnson for always being troopers and for providing transcription and other clerical tasks too numerous to mention.

And to my parents, grandparents, pastors, aunts, uncles, cousins, teachers, coaches, mentors, and friends for being a part of this process and a part of my life—your unwavering love, support, and encouragement have sustained me throughout the years.

CHAPTER 1

● ● ● ● ● ● ● ● ● ● ● ●

Give God the Glory

"All things are possible
for those who believe."
— Mark 9:23

"It's an attitude-is-everything day at Harrell Performance Systems! How can I help you?"

I answered the phone the way we always do at my office in Atlanta. It was after 5:30 on a wintry Wednesday evening in January of 1999, and my staff had already gone home. Usually at that hour I'd let the calls move on through to voice mail, but for some reason I decided to take this particular call.

I'm sure glad I did.

"This is Ellen Pollock from *The Wall Street Journal*," said the woman's voice on the other end of the line. "I'm calling to speak to Keith Harrell."

"This is Keith Harrell," I answered. "How can I help you?"

"We're thinking about doing a story on motivational speakers," she explained matter-of-factly, "and we were given your name. So I was wondering if I would be able to interview you?"

My response was one I don't think she'd heard before. I said, "*Give God the glory!* Thank you for calling!"

There was a brief moment of silence on the other end of the phone. Eventually she replied, "Uh, what did you just say?"

"I just want to give God all the honor and the glory," I repeated, as a broad smile spread across my face. "Now," I continued, "whether you actually write about *this* motivational speaker or not, God's gonna bless me because I'm giving Him all the glory."

Ellen regained her composure and began asking me questions about my life as a speaker. She inquired about my keynote message, entitled "Attitude Is Everything." She asked about its acceptance at some of the Fortune 500 companies where I present it. Before too long, she had a much better idea of who Keith Harrell was.

I must admit that I grew apprehensive as she inquired about the personal details of my life. Being a private person by nature, I was concerned about some of her questions—such as how much money I made, how many speeches I'd given over the last year, how many days I was on the road, and did I have a family.

As I answered her questions, I became more curious about Ellen Pollock.

"Tell me about yourself," I said to her, turning the table. I was pleased that she was willing to do so.

"My husband and I have a little baby girl in our lives," she responded with excitement in her voice. "We're so proud of her."

Ellen and I continued to have a pleasant conversation. She kept asking me about speaking, and I kept asking about her and her family.

"We're thinking about doing a story on motivational speakers," she repeated. "I contacted quite a few speakers' bureaus, and for some reason, every one I called suggested that I contact you."

"Why's that?" I asked.

"Because you represent someone who's out there doing it right."

We continued the interview for a few more minutes. After it seemed that she had what she was looking for, we ended our conversation on the same note that it began on.

"Well, Ellen, I thank God for this positive conversation, and remember that attitude is everything!"

I hung up the phone and sat in the silence of my office. The stillness provided the ideal atmosphere for me to reflect on what had just occurred.

My mind turned to a good friend of mine, Ralph Bianco. From the time I'd started my own business, he'd always told me, "Keith, if you could ever get an article in *The Wall Street Journal,* it would really help your business." I wasn't sure if I'd be mentioned in the article Ellen was working on, but it was nice to know that the speakers' bureaus, which play such an important role in my business, had a positive opinion of my work.

A couple of weeks went by without any word from Ellen. I was just beginning to think that nothing was going to come of the interview, when a phone call was put through to my office.

"Keith—hi, it's Ellen Pollock. I want to explain what's been going on up here."

"Great," I said.

"Well, I didn't tell you before, but this story was originally about the strange requests celebrity speakers make while out on the road."

"Really?" I asked.

"Yes. You know what I'm talking about," she continued. "Some like their hotel rooms set to a specific temperature, others like a particular beverage in the limousine that drives them from the airport, some like a certain brand of shampoo at their hotel."

We both laughed.

"Every speakers' bureau I called would give me a few anecdotes for the story, but for some reason, they'd change the subject and tell me I should talk to you, because you're making such a positive impact on the business community through your keynote speech."

"I remember you saying that."

"Well, I went home and told my husband about our conversation. While I was talking to him, I began to feel as if I were being *led* to change the direction of the story away from the celebrity angle, and instead tell the story about you and your impact on corporate America."

"Give God the glory," I said again. (I guess Ellen was getting used to it by now.) Then I thanked her for what she was going to do and assured her that I'd give her as much help as she needed.

Over the next few weeks, I learned about the efficiency and thoroughness of the research that goes into an article for *The Wall Street Journal*. Ellen was very good about checking facts, as well as the accuracy of my statements. She contacted business associates, customers, people who'd heard me speak, people I grew up with, friends, teachers, coaches, and all of my current office staff.

She even called my former high school basketball coach, Al Hairston, who decided to check with me before he made a statement.

"What's this all about, Keith?" Coach asked.

"I may be featured in an article in *The Wall Street Journal*," I replied.

Coach couldn't resist making a joke. After a pause he asked, "Do you want me to tell her you were good? Or do you want me to tell her the truth?"

Ellen even came to hear me speak at one of my engagements. I wanted her to see me while I was speaking to several thousand salespeople who were excited and filled with energy, but her schedule only allowed her to attend a speech in Cincinnati for a small group of managers. I was the closing speaker of their four-day event, so these folks were weary by the time I showed up.

Ellen sat in the front row—tape recorder in one hand, notepad in the other—listening, assessing, and evaluating my speech and the audience response. When I was introduced, the applause was weak compared to what a large national sales force could produce. I kept thinking, *I've got to kick it up a notch. Come on, folks, can you show me some love?*

They warmed up as my talk progressed—all 120 of them. They were a great audience, and I was pleased.

The interviews with Ellen continued, but one question was burning in my mind. I finally asked her, "What will be the *focus* of this article, anyway?" I tried to act as nonchalant as possible, but I really wanted to know the answer.

You see, I had some reservations. One friend had told me that sometimes reporters misrepresent people. I was also concerned about certain speakers' bureaus not being mentioned in the article. Ellen had told me she'd spoken to Nationwide Speakers Bureau, Leading Authorities Speakers Bureau, and the National Speakers Bureau, but I wanted her to interview some of the other major organizations that represent me. I wanted her to list them all because they all play an important role in the success of my business.

"Well, Keith, you know I'm not allowed to reveal that information to you," she replied to my surprise. "I don't even know for sure if this story will be printed once I write it," she went on. "There are no guarantees in this business."

"I see," I softly replied.

"My job is to gather all the information necessary to make this story work," she continued. "Then I pass on what I've done to the senior editors, who use as much or as little of it as they please. Even then, no one knows for sure what will go to print."

On Sunday evening, February 28, 1999, the phone rang at my home. It was Ellen Pollock with a fascinating little teaser: "Keith, if I were you, I'd be sure to pick up a copy of the *Journal* this Tuesday."

"Are you saying the article's going to be in this Tuesday's paper?"

"I can't say that," she replied, in the reporter's code I was beginning to understand. "Remember, I can't make any guarantees that the story will even run, but as I said, if I were you, I'd start looking on Tuesday."

"Is there *anything* you can tell me for sure?" I coaxed.

She paused, then said, "I can tell you that I've put the story to bed, meaning that I've turned over the article to my editors."

"So since you've put it to bed," I continued to prod, "*now* can you tell me what the story's about?"

"Keith, I'm sorry, but I still can't answer that question."

A new approach suddenly struck me: "I understand your limitations, but let me ask you another question, okay? Every time you've interviewed me, what have I talked about?"

"Well, you've talked mainly about three things: God, your church, and your pastor," she replied. "You've told me over and over how important your faith is and how blessed you are."

"So if you don't mention those things in the article, then obviously that article isn't about me."

"I hear you loud and clear," she said.

Before we hung up, I had one more issue I wanted to raise.

"Ellen, you know how the *Journal* draws those line sketches of people, instead of using photographs?"

"Sure, Keith, I know what you mean."

"Well, if the article *does* run and they use a sketch, could you set aside the original artwork?"

"I don't know what I can do, but I'll see," she answered.

"That's good."

"Why do you want it?" she asked.

I responded sincerely, "'Cause I want to give it to my mom."

▲ ▲ ▲

Tuesday, March 2, 1999, was a cold, blustery day in the Midwest. I was in Illinois staying at the Chicago Airport Marriott, for I was scheduled to make a presentation to about 500 executives of the Lincoln Financial Group later that morning. As is my routine when I'm on the road, one of the first things I did upon waking was to pray and thank God for giving me another day . . . and then I called to check my voice mail.

I had a message waiting that certainly caught my attention.

"Keith, it's Dr. Ed Metcalf. You need to call me at home *right away!*"

Dr. Ed is one of my mentors, but he rarely leaves me voice mail, so I called his home immediately.

"What's up, Dr. Ed?" I asked, trying to act as cool as possible.

"I'll tell you what's up, Keith," he replied excitedly. "Our friend Dr. Bill Cross just saw an article in today's *Journal*, so he faxed it on over to me . . . it's all about you!"

"No kidding?" I responded.

"The story is called 'The Selling of a Golden Speech,'" he continued. "The subtitle is 'On the Motivational Circuit, a Star with Attitude.'"

Right there on the phone, Dr. Ed started reading the entire article to me.

> Their bags are packed and stowed in the back of the room, and 120 executives of National City Mortgage Co. are ready to head home after three days of meetings in a Cincinnati hotel. Keith Harrell races to the front of the Versailles-style meeting room to give the closing address. The applause is polite. . . .

Suddenly I remembered the line sketch I wanted to give to my mom.

"Dr. Ed, " I interrupted, "tell me about the picture."

He didn't respond; instead, he just kept reading.

> Attitude Is Everything. That's the title of the speech, Mr. Harrell, a 43-year-old motivational speaker, is making today. He has given the same talk to employees of Coca-Cola Co., Microsoft Corp., and hundreds of other companies. . . .
>
> "There are over 4,000 professional speakers," says Mark French of Leading Authorities, a lecture agency. "Most of them are starving. There are a couple hundred who are doing well. There are probably 20 who are doing exceptionally well. Keith Harrell is doing exceptionally well."

"But Dr. Ed . . . did the line sketch turn out okay?"

"Keith, it doesn't look like they did a line sketch. There's a photograph."

"A photograph?" I asked.

"Yes . . . well, no. Actually, it's not *a* photograph. It's one big photograph accompanied by *four* smaller ones down the side of the article."

"There are five pictures of me in *The Wall Street Journal?*"

"That's right," he replied.

"How long is it?"

"Well, remember it's been faxed to me, so I can't really tell how long it is. But hang on—I'll finish reading it to you."

And with that, Dr. Ed took up where he'd left off.

He set up shop in his second bedroom, hired a neighbor to answer his phone and made speeches at schools. He hired a marketing consultant. He wrote a book based on his speech about attitude that was printed by a custom publisher, which sells his book primarily through him instead of through bookstores.

These days Mr. Harrell has a staff of four in Atlanta and a second home in Scottsdale, Ariz. He has sold 52,000 copies of his book. . . . Now Mr. Harrell faces the dilemma of how to build his business without running himself ragged. He traveled 200,000 miles last year and no longer speaks on weekends so he can attend his church, the 15,000-member, charismatic World Changers Ministries in College Park, Georgia.

I was pleased that Ellen had done such a thorough job and had made a point to include the name of my church in the article.

When Dr. Ed was done, I placed the phone on its cradle and immediately picked it up again—I just had to call my dad.

When I went into business, I always wanted my father to know that I could make it. As a retired business professor, I knew that my father would understand the significance of the article. It was 6:30 A.M. in Seattle, but I was excited.

"Dad, you've gotta get up!"

"What's wrong?" he asked, with worry in his voice.

"Nothing at all," I replied. "You just have to go out and buy yourself a copy of today's *Wall Street Journal*."

"Why?"

"'Cause there's a story about me on the first page of the second section!"

"Okay, Keith, I'm up," he replied. "I'm on my way out the door to buy me a paper."

Next I called my sister, who also lives in Seattle. "Toni, wake up! Wake up!" I implored. Since she's a retired police captain, she probably thought a crime had taken place. But before she could jump to the wrong conclusion, I once again blurted out: "I'm in today's *Wall Street Journal!*"

"Really? That's awesome!"

She ended up driving to three different places before she could find a copy, but when she found it, she bought *ten*. She spent the morning dropping off copies all over town. She took one to her church and hung a copy on the bulletin board. She went into the pastor's office and gave him his own personal copy. And then she spent the rest of the day visiting with friends and sharing the news.

Then it was time to call another important member of my family . . . my mother.

"Mom?" I said, as she answered the phone in her Seattle office. It was still early, but my mother was already at work.

"Hi! How you doin'?" she said.

"You've got to go out and get today's paper, 'cause I'm in it!"

"Why are you in the Seattle paper?"

"No, Mom, I'm in *The Wall Street Journal*," I replied.

"*The Journal Wall?*" she asked, with obvious confusion.

I smiled on the other end of the phone, suddenly realizing that my dear mom was not familiar with *The Wall Street Journal*.

"Write this down, Mom," I instructed, as I spelled out, "W-A-L-L-space-S-T-R-E-E-T . . . "

"All right, honey, I've got it," she responded.

"It should be right outside your building at the newsstand,"

I went on. "Go out and get a copy."

I hung up, waited a little while, and then called her back because I was so curious to hear what she thought. I called and called and called, but I was put through to her voice mail every time.

Later that night, I finally connected with her at her home. "Where were you all day, Mom?"

"I went from office to office, floor to floor, making certain *everyone* in the building knew that my son was in *The Wall Street Journal*."

▲ ▲ ▲

After speaking with Mom at work that morning, I finished getting ready for my presentation and headed down the elevator at the Chicago Airport Marriott. Making certain I had enough time for a little detour, I found the hotel gift shop and tried my best to wander in casually. Hands in my pockets, trying to look as if I didn't have anything particular in mind, I strolled over to the newsstand, where I saw what I was after. I counted a dozen papers in the stack and stopped to ponder the situation. If I took them all, no one else would have the opportunity to see why I was excited, so I decided to buy only three of them, leaving plenty for others. (Plus, I knew I'd be hitting every newsstand between here and the airport as soon as my speech was over.)

As I stepped up to pay for the papers, the clerk looked at me quizzically. "*Three* copies of the same paper?" she asked.

"Yeah," I responded with a sheepish grin. "There's an article in here about a very good friend of mine."

"That's nice," she replied. "Let me see it."

As soon as I turned to the front page of the second section, the woman saw five photos of the man standing before her. She couldn't contain her enthusiasm. "Hey, everybody, look over here!" she said to the three or four others who were browsing in the gift shop. "This guy's in today's paper!"

Before long, several copies had been sold.

Once out of the shop, I made my way to the ballroom where Lincoln Financial Group awaited my presentation. I'm always excited to be in front of an audience, but on that particular day my enthusiasm reached a new level. I was in the zone—bringing the crowd to laughter, causing them to think, and giving them key strategies on how to maintain a positive attitude.

At the appropriate moment, I told them my news. "You never know when something positive and exciting is gonna catch you off guard," I began. The crowd nodded its agreement. "I received a very wonderful surprise when I woke up this morning," I continued.

The audience leaned in as I paused long enough to whet their appetites. "There are some folks who wrote a very positive story about my speaking on 'Attitude' to corporations like yours. And it's in today's *Wall Street Journal!*"

At that precise moment, I held up the article for the crowd to see.

They looked skeptical, and I could tell they didn't believe me. I suppose they thought it was a normal part of my presentation and that it wasn't for real—they must have figured I printed up a mock version of the paper just to make my point.

But all that changed a few minutes later. Unbeknownst to me, one of the members of the audience had slipped out of the ballroom and bought a copy of the *Journal* at the gift shop. I guess he'd decided to check up on me to see if I was telling the truth. It didn't take him long to find what he was looking for:

"HEY EVERYBODY, HE REALLY IS IN *THE WALL*

STREET JOURNAL!" the guy bellowed out to the entire crowd of his co-workers.

The crowd exploded into spontaneous applause.

When the speech was over, I shook some hands, met some folks, and then headed back to my room. I spent the next few hours attempting to call my office to alert my staff about the article. All of our phone lines were jammed the entire day with people calling in response to the *Journal*'s story.

There were all types of messages waiting for me. I heard from speakers' bureaus who wanted to know if I'd consider working with them, and I heard from prospective customers who were interested in having me speak to their groups. I heard from publishers who were calling to communicate their interest in me . . . even when they'd previously rejected my book. I also heard from several literary agents who were calling to offer their services in helping me place my book with a major publishing house.

But my favorite messages came from the people in my past. People with whom I'd attended elementary school were calling to reacquaint themselves with me. Friends I went to high school with were calling to congratulate me. Fellow alumni from my college were calling to express their pride. Colleagues from my days at IBM called to offer their encouragement.

My friend Reggie Green wanted to know why I hadn't called to tell him the article was going to run. The truth was that I'd hesitated to call any of my friends, concerned that they'd think I was boasting.

While I was flying home that evening, I finally had the opportunity to read the article for myself. When I finished, a man from across the aisle leaned over and congratulated me on being in the paper. All I could say was "Give God the glory!"

When I got home, I called my buddy Ralph Bianco, whom I hadn't spoken to for quite some time. I just wanted to share the good news with him.

It was a wonderful time for me to reflect on all that had taken place in my life. Sitting in my living room, I once again thanked God for using me in such a significant way . . .

. . . *The Wall Street Journal* . . . The Selling of a Golden Speech . . . The Star with Attitude . . . A Major Speaking Career . . .

Could all this be happening to the same person who was once a shy, skinny kid who stuttered?

▲ ▲ ▲

LESSON 1:
Do the Right Thing
▲ ▲ ▲ ▲ ▲ ▲ ▲ ▲ ▲

Professionalism coupled with a positive attitude, a passion for work, and a personal vision executed with integrity is what I call "doing the right thing."

The Wall Street Journal discovered me because my name kept surfacing among speakers' bureaus as "someone who's doing everything right." I've come to realize that wherever we are, whatever we're doing, someone, somewhere, is taking note. In my case, it was the bureaus that represent me, and book engagements. In your case, it could be an employer, a subordinate, your children, or a potential client. You never know who's looking. A vision can't fail if you do the right thing.

The most critical first step is understanding your purpose in life and developing a personal vision. A personal vision consists of knowing what you want to do, for whom, and for what purpose. Developing this vision is often a very difficult and time-consuming process in which you'll discover that successfully executing it requires personal sacrifice.

Having a personal vision enabled me to endure the lack of support I encountered when I first went into business for myself. It helped me overcome the naysayers who told me, "People won't respond to your message. It's not important—it's fluff."

Passion comes easier when you're doing what you want and are fulfilling your purpose and vision for your life. When you have a passion for your work, you can get up early and work late. You can make the hundreds and hundreds of phone calls and travel away from home and family. It even helps you through times when the rewards come in every form *but* money.

When you're doing the right thing, your attitude is upbeat and positive and your integrity is never in question. Serving your customers is what you do, and quality of service is paramount to how you do your work.

In my profession, there are many excellent speakers—the difference for *The Wall Street Journal* was that I consistently did things *right!*

Doing the right thing—with purpose, passion, integrity, and the right attitude—will always get you noticed.

CHAPTER 2

. . . .

"I'm Too Tall, I Can't Talk, I Don't Fit!"

*"Teach your children to
choose the right path,
and when they are older
they will remain upon it."*
— Proverbs 22:6

There's a lot more to my story than was in *The Wall Street Journal*'s article in 1999. . . .

I guess I've always been excited about life, because I was born at Columbus Hospital in Seattle, Washington, two weeks before I was due. My parents went to a scheduled appointment with the obstetrician one cold December day around 12:30 in the afternoon, but after a quick examination of my mother, the doctor made a surprise announcement: "Take this woman to the hospital—it's time!"

Just over an hour later, I was born. My dad's mother was the nurse in charge of the newborn nursery at Columbus Hospital, so I know we got the red-carpet treatment. Grandma wheeled me over to the nursery and placed me in the front row so that everyone who passed by the window could see her new grandson.

My mom was ready to go home the very next day (she'd had an equally easy labor a year and a half earlier with my sister, Toni), so they released us and we headed to the Rainier Vista Housing Projects in Seattle, where we were living while Dad finished up school. A short time later, we all moved in with my maternal grandmother. Her house on 33rd Avenue would be my home until I was three.

But my folks didn't start out in Washington State. They were both born in Louisiana—my dad in New Orleans and my mom in Saline. Dad made his way to the Pacific Northwest and settled in Bremerton, Washington, before moving to Seattle. My mother's family also moved to Seattle, arriving in 1948. In 1949, my parents met, fell in love, and married.

My dad dropped out of the University of Washington during his freshman year at the age of 19. He simply wasn't focused on school, so he spent the following year working sporadically as a construction worker. He soon became skilled as a wood, wire, and metal lather. Today, because of prefabricated construction components such as Sheetrock, there isn't a need for this type of skilled labor, but in the 1950s, walls were still built with lath and plaster.

Dad worked as a lather off and on for ten years, supporting his family and attending college. His older brother had graduated from college, and both of his grandfathers were college educated. My dad was motivated to finish school because he wanted to provide a better quality of life for his family. After he got his degree, my father entered the field of education. For 36 years he taught business and accounting courses at Seattle Central Community College.

Shortly after I was born, my mom went to work for

Boeing—a job she held from 1956 through 1970. She then went to work for the city of Seattle, where she was employed for 29 years. At the time of her retirement, she was an asset manager for the Department of Housing.

Right around my fourth birthday, we moved from my grandmother's house to our own place at 1208 26th Avenue. My memories of life as a toddler and preschooler are generally happy. According to my mom, I *always* had a basketball with me . . . under my arm, dribbling, passing, or shooting. My sister, Toni, says she sometimes saw me playing kickball or riding a scooter, but as far back as *I* can recall, it was all about basketball.

Another thing I remember is that I didn't like being teased. When I was about five years old, my Aunt Sue gave me a present. I was excited about receiving a gift—until I opened it and discovered a pair of blue-and-white-striped coveralls with the proverbial flap on the back seat. The only other people I had seen wearing pants like those were milkmen, who were delivering milk and eggs to our doorstep back then.

I hated those pants. The neighborhood kids made fun of me every time I wore them. I didn't like the way I looked in them, and I didn't like the way I felt in them. "Don't make me wear the milkman pants," I remember pleading with my mom and my aunt.

I thought wearing those pants was a challenge, but I was about to face an even bigger one . . . I stuttered.

▲ ▲ ▲

No one in my family ever laughed at me because of my stuttering. My mother would always say, "Keith, your brain is moving faster than your mouth. Slow down and take your time."

But on the first day of kindergarten, life completely changed for me. Mom came into my bedroom early that morning and said, "Honey, you've gotta get up. It's the first day of school."

I was so excited that I jumped out of bed.

"I set out two pairs of pants for you," Mom explained. "One pair of jeans and one pair of corduroys. You can pick the pair you want to wear today."

She left me alone with my dilemma. I came up with the only answer I could think of . . . I put on both pairs of pants.

When my mom came back in the bedroom, she smiled. "Keith, you've got to make a decision, honey. I know you like both pairs, so listen. You can wear one pair today and the other pair tomorrow. How's that?"

I grinned and nodded. I went with the corduroys 'cause I thought I looked *cute* in them. Plus, I liked the noise they made when I walked. *Swish, swish, swish* went my pants as I strolled out to the car with Mom.

We drove up to the front of Stevens Elementary School, and I remember thinking that it looked enormous. We had to climb several stairs to get to my classroom, and for a five-year-old, it felt as if we'd gone up 37 flights by the time we arrived at Room 106.

Mom and I entered the classroom, and I began looking around at all the boys and girls who would be my classmates. Our names were written on cards placed on our desks. I was thrilled to see that my desk was right up front—first row.

It was time for Mom to leave, and I'll never forget the image of her standing in the classroom doorway, a tiny tear in her eye as she blew me a kiss good-bye. I waved back, overwhelmed by all the excitement school had to offer.

When I think back on all of the people who've made a positive impact on my life, one of the first names that comes to mind is my kindergarten teacher, Miss Peterson. She possessed an enthusiasm that was contagious, and she could light up a room with her smile.

"Boys and girls, I'm the happiest teacher in the whole world," Miss Peterson began that morning. "Do you know why?"

We all shook our heads.

"Because I have the best students in the world!"

We all sat up a little straighter at our desks.

"What I'd like to do is go around the room," Miss Peterson continued enthusiastically, "and one by one, I want each and every one of you to stand up. When you do so, I want you to stand tall and say your name as loud as you can. Now . . . who wants to be first?"

Her eyes circled the room several times before finally focusing on mine. She bent down closer to me and asked, "Would you go first for Miss Peterson? Come on, sweetie, you can do it, stand up."

I jumped up, turned around to face the class, and said, "M-m-m-m-m-y . . . n-n-n-n-n-ame . . ."

No words would come out. It was just like talking at home, but now there was no one to remind me, "Everything's okay, Keith. Just slow down and take your time." Instead, all I could hear was snickering as the other kids made fun of me.

Nancy, a girl with glasses, got up and announced to the class: "He can't talk—he can't even say his name. . . . He needs *help*."

Then a little boy named Billy looked me over and added, "You're too tall. You don't fit. You oughtta go home—you're too big for this class."

I sat back down at my desk. I felt rejected, like a loser. It was a kind of pain that I'd never experienced before. I remember wanting only two things at that moment: I wanted to hear the other students say their names, but more important, I wanted my mom.

As much as I tried to listen to everyone else, I couldn't hear a thing. Over and over in my mind those negative messages replayed: *You're too tall. You don't fit. You oughtta go home!*

By morning recess I'd had enough. My classmates marched out to the playground, and I ran home to Mom. (This was no small feat, for I lived almost two miles from the school.) As I sprinted up the steps of my front porch, I saw that Mom was already out of the house, and her arms were outstretched toward me. She gave me the tightest hug—exactly what I needed.

"Mama, I'm too tall . . . I can't talk . . . I don't fit," I explained. "All the kids laughed at me."

My mom reassured me. "Everything's going to be all right, sweetie. Mama just got off the phone with Miss Peterson. Mama knows how you feel."

I immediately felt better. She understood.

"I want you to know that I'm proud of you," she went on. "Do you know why?"

"Why?" I asked.

"Because you *tried*."

It was so good to know that Mom was on my side.

"We're going to work hard, we're going to stay focused, and we're going to get you some help. Mama's going to work with you every single day, because one day, my little man's going to stand tall and say his name as loud and as well as the other boys and girls."

Not long after that, Mom bought me a tape recorder. As I moved along through elementary school, she'd tape me reading out loud and then play it back for me. I loved it when she'd play tapes where I read well, so I could hear what I sounded like when I did it right. She wanted me to learn the feeling of succeeding at my task.

My grandmother was another wise woman who would encourage me with a helpful comparison. My uncle, Dr. Bill

Harrell, had endured the same stuttering problem when he was young. My uncle was very bright, and he graduated from the University of Washington when he was only 19. He recently retired from Texas Southern University, where he was a pharmacy professor for more than 50 years.

"You're gonna be just like your uncle," she'd encourage. "He grew out of it, and so will you."

"I b-b-b-believe you, Grandma," I'd reply.

"But your uncle practiced," she'd continue. "He wouldn't take it personally when people made fun of him. He just practiced and practiced and really worked at it."

I was sure that Grandma had all the answers. She often quoted them right from her big, worn-out Bible, which she was always reading. So I really did believe her. And I took her literally. Every year I'd grow taller, and I'd figure I was that much closer to outgrowing my stuttering. I just knew it was a matter of time before I'd grow out of it for good.

Of course she actually meant, "When you get *older,* you won't have to stutter." But I was hearing, "When you get *taller,* you won't have to stutter." My grandmother's words gave me confidence. And her assessment of the situation definitely had merit—most children between the ages of two and five experience some degree of stuttering as they learn to speak, but for reasons still unknown, only one in four continues to stutter beyond adolescence. (While there's still no clear answer as to why more than three million Americans stutter, much has been learned in the 50 years since the Stuttering Foundation of America was established. For example, males are four times more likely than females to stutter, and children who stutter are no more likely to have psychological problems than children who do not. They're just as intelligent and well adjusted as non-stutterers. It's reassuring to know that many well-known individuals have overcome the challenges of stuttering—Winston Churchill, Marilyn Monroe, Carly Simon, James Earl Jones, Bob Love, Bill Walton, Ben Johnson, Senator Joseph Biden, Bo Jackson, Greg Louganis, John Stossel, and John F. Welch, to name a few.)

I can remember one of the first times I got angry at myself for stuttering. Whenever I went with my sister and my cousins, Bruce and Clayton (who was nicknamed "Peanut"), to Grandma's house, she always had some chores for us to do. She wanted us to learn the value of work, and if we worked hard, she'd reward us by giving us an allowance or by taking us to the store to buy candy.

One Saturday when I was visiting Grandma, she asked me to do a project that was new to me. "Keith, I want you to weed the garden," she said.

"Okay, Grandma," I replied obediently. But I had *no idea* how to weed a garden. I couldn't tell a weed from a plant, so I just started pulling up whatever was in front of me. I got bored pretty quickly, so I went back to the house.

"I'm done," I announced as I walked in the door.

"You are?" she asked in amazement.

"Yep, I'm all finished, Grandma."

She walked out of the house, took one look at the garden, and began shaking her head. "Honey, I thought you could do a much better job than this," she said. "I'm disappointed in you."

I tried to explain my confusion, but I was getting excited, and that caused me to begin stuttering.

"Don't start stuttering now," she said. "I want you to do a better job. You need to finish the job you started."

By now I was feeling desperate, because I couldn't tell her that *I didn't know what to do.* I couldn't talk.

She kept saying, "Slow down—take your time."

"Y-y-y-you n-n-n-need to explain it to m-m-m-me. Y-y-y-you s-s-s-show m-m-m-me," I pleaded. But I couldn't get it out. In total frustration, I turned around and ran home. I wasn't upset with Grandma; I was angry with myself because I wanted to do better, but I couldn't communicate to her that I needed more instruction.

I felt pretty certain that when I got home I was going to be in trouble, because as I was running away, Grandma was calling to me, "Come back here, boy! Come back here! Do you hear me talking to you?" But to my surprise, neither Mom nor Dad ever said anything to me about the garden, so I'm convinced that Grandma never told them about the incident. She knew I was disappointed and upset and I just couldn't express myself.

Many nights I'd lie in bed praying, asking God, "Why did You make me so tall? Why did You make me stutter? How come I can't talk like the other kids?"

▲ ▲ ▲

LESSON 2:
Keep Your Self-Image Mirror Clean
▲ ▲ ▲ ▲ ▲ ▲ ▲ ▲ ▲

When was the first time you ever felt different? For me it was that first day in kindergarten. The message I received was that I was too tall, I couldn't talk, and I didn't belong. Children and adults can be cruel when someone doesn't fit their image of perfection. My self-image was clouded by others' perceptions of me. I thank God that my family, teachers, and friends looked beyond the pimples, long skinny legs, and stuttering to see my potential.

It's funny, but as I look back at my friends, they all had shortcomings; some were lesser and some were greater than mine. William had one glass eye, and LeeRoy had very poor dental care. But we didn't dwell on our disadvantages.

Through the acceptance of my family and friends, I began to understand that I was a unique individual. I had to clean my self-image mirror. I had to wipe away the negative message and come to the realization that God doesn't make junk! He's the Master Artisan, and He specializes in originals.

We all need to be reminded of this truth. From infancy to adulthood, our parents, teachers, and peers, along with messages relayed by television and advertisements, program us to believe that there's an ideal way to look and behave in order to be accepted. As an adult, I allowed others to keep me from applying for positions with IBM. I believed them when they told me that I didn't have the right back-ground or the proper credentials for certain positions. My degree was in community service and sociology, not business or marketing, so of course I thought they were right. The truth is that I was qualified to apply and compete for those positions and promotions. I just needed some Windex. How about you? What message from your past is keeping you from seeing your potential?

We're all made in the image of greatness; there-fore, we're all predestined for special things. The sooner you accept the fact that there will never be another you—that you're unique and set apart—the more confident you'll become in making choices that support your dreams and desires.

Remember, *you* are in control of your self-image. When others try to cloud your reflection with negatives, wipe off your self-image mirror so you can see yourself as God sees you—created to fulfill a divine purpose.

CHAPTER 3

A Student with "Special Needs"

"Love enures long and
is patient and kind."
— 1 Corinthians 13:4

B y the time I entered first grade, I'd been tested by, and assigned to, the school's speech therapist—in other words, I was a student with "special needs". Although I was labeled a "moderate" stutterer (one who stutters when excited or nervous), it seemed that any emotion could trigger it.

Stuttering was painful and embarrassing—I felt as if I had an incurable disease. Consequently, I became aloof and didn't want to participate in any classroom activities because I knew I'd have to speak. I thought that if I didn't stutter, the other kids wouldn't laugh at me. But even keeping my mouth shut didn't stop the teasing.

My first-grade teacher had a method of reminding us of our appointments without disturbing the rest of the class: She had a clock made out of construction paper tacked up in the front of the class, right by the name of the student. In my case, under the name *Keith* was a paper clock with the big hand on the 12 and the little hand on the 10. When 10 A.M. arrived, I'd slowly walk up to the front of the classroom, remove the thumbtacks, take the paper clock off the wall, and walk out the door. That's when my classmates would mock me, saying, "Go on, Keith— go and learn how to talk!"

Their words pierced like arrows.

I thank God for my speech therapist, who seemed to understand my pain. She was patient, kind, and encouraging, and she really loved what she did. "This is where you're going to get your help, Keith," she'd tell me in her soothing voice. "I want you to relax."

We'd go over a number of vocal exercises—such as taking breaths at the right time and slowing the pace at which I talked. We'd break each word down into syllables, and I'd work on relaxing my vocal muscles.

"Take your time," she'd often remind me. "Sound out the word. . . . control your tongue."

She'd say a word directly in my ear, put her hand on my mouth to show me how to move my lips, and then help me pronounce the word correctly. We also did visualization exercises, during which I'd try to "see" the words in my mind. We'd break a word down into parts and read them out loud, over and over—sometimes spending an entire hour on one syllable. And we'd work on the sounds that gave me the most difficulty—the *p*'s, the *s*'s, and the *t*'s.

She'd ask me, "What did you eat for dinner last night?" or "Are you playing basketball this weekend?" so that I'd feel comfortable engaging in a conversation. "Speak slowly, just like you were talking to yourself," she'd encourage.

That piece of advice was especially helpful to me, since I'd already begun the practice of having conversations with myself. I used to talk to myself each day when I walked home from school, and I enjoyed doing it. Why? Because when I talked to myself, I seldom stuttered. Sometimes I'd get home from school, go to my room, and continue the "dialogue." I liked the way I sounded when I did this. Before you conclude that I was totally crazy, remember that I was doing exactly what my speech therapist had told me to do. I was practicing. It probably sounds weird, but this routine really helped.

I did everything I could to avoid claiming the label of "stutterer"—but when I was back in class and the teacher would announce, "Class, it's time to read out loud," the pain would return.

Everyone would look at me and giggle. They all knew how much I hated this part of the day, yet they couldn't resist laughing at my expense. "Pick Keith! Pick Keith!" they'd yell excitedly, volunteering me to go first. They did this for two reasons: First, they knew I was too stubborn and determined to quit— I'd stand up there all day if that's how long it took to read. And that's the second reason . . . *it took all day.*

They knew that if I was chosen to read out loud, no one else would have to read that day. I'd eat up the entire period plodding through the assigned material.

Sometimes I could get the next day's reading assignment ahead of time. I'd go home those afternoons and read aloud over and over and over again in my bedroom. The practice would be of some help the next day, but the stuttering was always there. If a word began with a *p* or an *s*, I'd pretend I didn't know it. It was less embarrassing for me to be thought of as stupid than a stutterer.

Stuttering even started to affect my spiritual life. My family worshiped at the First African Methodist Episcopal (AME)

Church in Seattle. When I reached third grade, my mom began dropping me off for Sunday school, which was an hour and 45 minutes before the worship service.

My Sunday-school teacher was fond of having students stand to read the scriptures, but for me this presented a problem. I genuinely wanted to listen and learn about God, but the thought of reading out loud and enduring more teasing from my peers was more than I could bear . . . so I began ditching.

My mom would drop me off in front of the church, and I'd go in one door and out the other. I'd hang out at the corner store or walk around, always being very mindful of the time. When it was time for the morning service to begin, I'd always be right back by the front door of the church, waiting for my mom, just as we had prearranged. No one ever knew I skipped Sunday school (that is, until now).

▲ ▲ ▲

The only time that I could really forget about my stuttering was when I played sports. I especially loved basketball and baseball, and I seemed to excel at them. But best of all, they didn't require any talking. Of course, I could "chatter" on the baseball diamond like everyone else—"Come on, baby, come on b-b-baby! You can't hit! You're gonna s-strike out!"—because chatter sounded like stuttering anyway.

When I was nine years old, some of the older guys in the neighborhood dragged me along to Little League tryouts, and before I knew it, I was on the team. Because I was one of the youngest boys who made the cut, I was very proud of my accomplishment—despite the fact that I sat on the bench for most of the season and only got a partial uniform.

I wanted everyone to know I was on a team . . . not just *any* team, but the Lawyers Title Little League team. Lawyers Title was our sponsor, and we wore our uniforms proudly. My mother tells me that I *never* took my cap off. I wore it everywhere: around the house, to school, to bed. Mom would have to come in after I'd fallen asleep to remove it from my head. Hey, my team had a winning tradition, and I wanted everyone to know that the tradition included me.

But more important to me than winning was the encouragement I received from my coach, Sarge. He really loved mentoring us kids; he'd show up early at practice and stay late, helping anyone who wanted to improve their skills. He was one of the first men to really inspire me.

Sarge was convinced that I could become a good ballplayer, so he put me in the outfield and hit fly balls to me. I was no good at judging distance, so I constantly missed them. They'd either fall in front of me or fly way over my head. But Sarge was always there with uplifting words. He'd hit those fly balls and then yell, "Get on your horse, Keith! Get on your horse!"

I'd run as fast as I could, scooping up the ball from the ground and throwing it back into him. I wasn't very good, but I could hustle. I showed the other guys a positive attitude, and Sarge loved it.

"You're not going to be playing a lot this year," he told me, "but you're just as important as anyone else in this dugout."

I smiled wide.

"By encouraging and cheering everyone else along, you're a key part of this team. You understand?"

"Yes, Coach," I replied.

"You keep hustling, you keep learning, you keep practicing," he urged, "and one day you'll be on the all-star team."

I never forgot those words.

Sarge was right: I hardly played that year. The next year I got a little more playing time, but by the time I was 11, I was starting—and at the end of that season, I *was* chosen to be on the all-star team.

▲ ▲ ▲

Encouragement was so important to me in those growing-up years. People like Sarge and my speech therapist kept planting the seed in my mind that I was improving, even though *I* didn't feel like I was at the time. They kept marking my improvement and urging me to continue practicing.

But there's another inspirational person I must add to my list—my fifth-grade teacher, Mr. Twine.

There weren't many African-American or male teachers at the school, so Mr. Twine was a unique guy. He was a big man, and he was strong. He was also very strict, which caused many of my classmates to think he was mean. But I knew he was doing what he needed to do to keep our attention and to make sure we learned. He loved us all; that's why he pushed us. He had high expectations and wanted all of us to succeed.

Mr. Twine taught me to have confidence in myself, which was a lesson I really wanted to learn. For example, he helped me see my height as an advantage, not a disadvantage. Whenever the class was headed out for an assembly, a fire drill, or recess, he'd announce, "All right, class, form a single line. That's right, everyone behind Keith!"

Then he'd turn to me and explain: "You're the tallest, so you're going to lead us outside. We'll all be able to see you. I'll be in the back, making sure everyone follows."

He knew I'd be the easiest person to line up behind since I was so tall, but he also knew that choosing me as the leader would motivate me. Most of my other teachers would put me in the back of the line, but Mr. Twine used my height in a positive way.

"Look up at Keith," he'd tell the class. "Just follow him."

Thanks, Mr. Twine, for your patience in building my confidence and self-esteem.

▲ ▲ ▲

I had friends who believed in me as well. Guys like LeeRoy Clayton, Jr.; Delo Hayes; my cousin Peanut; and William Booker helped me survive some awkward times growing up. I can still recall a magic moment that year when LeeRoy and I were in Mr. Twine's class . . . Valentine's Day.

Sports normally took up most of my free time, but in the fifth grade, baseball and basketball met some fierce competition from the opposite sex. Actually, one girl in particular caught my eye—her name was Renee Johnson.

Since I hadn't "grown out" of my stuttering yet, I was too shy to let Renee know how I felt. I couldn't talk, especially around girls. All my friends were starting to notice the females, so with Valentine's Day approaching, I decided it was time to get into the game.

"LeeRoy," I whispered one morning before class began, "I need some advice from you."

"What's up?" he replied.

"You know Renee Johnson?"

"Yeah."

"I like her," I confessed. "I want her to be my valentine."

"So call her up," he suggested.

"Call her?" I gasped in horror.

"That's right. Tell her you're interested and ask if she'll go out with you."

I started backpedaling. "I don't know . . ."

"Look, it's easy," he countered. "Tell you what—after school today, come over to my house and watch me. I'll call my girlfriend, Alicia, and ask her to be my valentine. She'll have Renee's phone number. You'll see—there's nothing to it."

With LeeRoy tutoring me, I didn't know how this plan could fail. As soon as the afternoon bell rang, we raced back to LeeRoy's house, and he placed the call to his girlfriend.

"Alicia?" he cooed over the phone. "This is LeeRoy."

I couldn't hear what she said, but I could tell from the smile on LeeRoy's face that things had started off well.

"I want to ask you a question," he told her. "Would you be my valentine?"

The expression on his face made it quite clear that she had responded positively. LeeRoy said good-bye and hung up the phone . . . quite simple, really. I was impressed with his confidence, plus he was so smooth. I decided to give it a shot.

LeeRoy dialed Renee's phone number as I looked on nervously. Confidence coursed through my body—until the phone stopped ringing. There, on the other end, was the sweet voice of Renee.

"Hello?" she said.

I froze. My heart was thumping so hard that I thought it was going to pound right out of my chest. My tongue was all tied up in knots. I tried to say her name, but I couldn't get past the first consonant. In my panic, I struggled to recall one or two exercises from my speech therapy, but none of them worked.

"R-r-r-r-r-r," I stammered, completely locked up.

I hung up the phone. I was so frustrated, so devastated. Why couldn't I do it like LeeRoy?

But my good buddy was not going to let me quit.

"That was good, Keith," LeeRoy assured me. "You're almost there! You can't stop now. She knows it was you on the phone, so she's waiting for you to call back. You've got to call her back, Keith—she *wants* to be your valentine."

"You really think she wants to be my valentine?" I asked LeeRoy. It was hard for me to believe.

"Oh, yeah," he prompted. "You'd better call her back. That's all I can say."

Somehow the fact that LeeRoy believed in me gave me the motivation to call Renee back. This time I got a little more than halfway through her first name before my stuttering kicked in.

"Ren-n-n-n-n . . ."

I was just about ready to hang up once again when LeeRoy took matters into his own hands. Snatching the phone out of my grasp, he said, "Renee, this is LeeRoy. Keith is trying to say that he wants you to be his valentine, okay? We'll be bringing your valentine to school tomorrow. Bye now . . . wait! Keith wants to say good-bye, too."

"Bye, Ren-n-e-e-e."

What a friend I had in LeeRoy. I don't think I would have had the courage to call Renee back after that first failed attempt without LeeRoy standing there supporting me. He cared enough to walk me through what could have been a very traumatic moment in my social life . . . plus he got me together with Renee, who was really fun. Yet my true love was still *basketball*.

▲ ▲ ▲

LESSON 3:
Be a Gatekeeper
▲ ▲ ▲ ▲ ▲ ▲ ▲ ▲ ▲

Do you remember that old rhyme, "Sticks and stones may break my bones but words can never hurt me"? The sticks and stones part is definitely true . . . they hurt—but so do words! Planted in your spirit, words take root and either nourish or strangle your dreams and ambitions. Yes, we all know that words can cause unbearable pain—either self-inflicted (as was the case when I replayed the taunts of my schoolmates), or in the form of unsolicited comments from well-meaning individuals.

In the Old Testament, the Levites were given the responsibility of being gatekeepers to the house of the Lord. The main guards would spend the night stationed around the house of God because they had to protect it.

We, too, need to be gatekeepers and watch what we allow in our minds—we need to be on guard 24/7. The next time someone says something negative to you, block it. Defend your passageways. Filter negative input by protecting yourself from what you hear, say, and see. You don't have to own everything you hear. Don't feed your spirit negative thoughts by viewing unpleasant, distracting, or graphically disturbing images. Don't engage in conversations with others (or with yourself) that depress or defeat your spirit.

I wish that as a young person I'd internalized more of the messages I received from Sarge, my coach; Mr. Twine, my teacher; and my friends, who saw my positive attributes and focused on them. Instead, I only replayed the taunts of my schoolmates—a habit that caused me to miss wonderful opportunities to learn and grow.

Don't let anyone cause you to miss your blessings! Your mouth, your eyes, and your ears are the gates to your heart—guard them! As a gatekeeper, block negative words, speak life-affirming statements, and engage in uplifting conversations. Let the next words you speak be ones of inspiration . . . to yourself *and* to everyone you meet.

CHAPTER 4

Practice Makes Improvement

"Now we ask you, brothers, to respect those
who work hard among you . . ."
— 1 Thessalonians 5:12

My love affair with basketball started very early for a very obvious reason . . . I was always the tallest kid around. And I kept growing—by the end of sixth grade, I was 6' 2"; when I finished eighth grade, I measured in at 6' 4".

I liked being tall, but it sometimes brought about challenges. For example, people always thought I was older than I really was. Even back in kindergarten, kids who weren't in my class thought I was in the third grade. And then, when I was nine, I went with two of my older cousins, Steve and Michael, to a Boy Scout meeting. The man in charge took one look at me and invited me to join the local troop. The only problem was that I was supposed to be a Cub Scout because of my age. But since I was as tall as the other 12-year-olds, the leader assumed I was old enough—and I became a Boy Scout.

I stayed with the Boy Scouts for a short time, got my uniform, and attended the meetings. Then guilt set in, because I realized I hadn't done what was right. So I told the scoutmaster my true age . . . and happily joined the Cub Scouts.

But not everyone believed me when I said that I was younger than I looked. By the time I was 11, I was finding it harder and harder to convince people that I was still just a sixth-grader. This really started to put a damper on one of my favorite pastimes—going to the movies.

Anyone under 12 could buy a movie ticket for half the adult price. I'd stand in line and then I'd step forward, lean down to speak into the little hole in the glass, and tell the clerk, "One child's ticket, please."

He'd look at me and smirk. "No way, kid."

"Why not?" I'd ask.

"Because there's no way you're under 12."

"I know how old I am—I'm 11," I'd respond.

He'd just shake his head. "I'm not going to fall for that. Ain't no way you're 11."

One day I went home and told my mom what had been going on. "Next time you go to the movies, I'm going to give you a little something to take down there with you. Then they'll believe you," she smiled.

"What are you going to give me?" I asked.

"I'll just give you a copy of your birth certificate—that should do it!"

And she was right. For the rest of that year, the only way I could get into the movie theater for half price was if I flashed that copy of my birth certificate.

But when all was said and done, my height connected me with basketball—and that sport helped me bond with my dad.

Before we had basketball, my dad and I took fishing trips

to Moses Lake. We'd make the three-hour drive, and Dad would teach me how to bait my hook, put the bobber on, cast the line, and reel in the catch—just like his father had taught him. These remain some of the best memories of my life.

Another routine Dad and I looked forward to was measuring my height. Dad would have me stand in a doorway, and he'd put a little chip in the paint by the top of my head to mark my growth. We'd check it out every couple of months to see if I'd grown another quarter, half, or full inch.

Dad would encourage me by anticipating my growth. He'd say things like, "Next month I expect you'll be another half inch taller." Those words made me feel good about growing.

My father had some rough edges, however, and one of them was being extremely frugal with his money. I remember begging and pleading for him to buy me a bicycle, to no avail. I smile as I think back on some of those conversations:

"Dad, I need a new bike."

"No, you don't."

"Dad, I'm 12 years old. I'm 6' 2". I've had this bike since I was five!" (This was no exaggeration—the bike I had was one my grandmother had bought me years ago, and I'd long since outgrown it.)

"I'll just raise the seat and get you some higher handlebars," he'd say. "It's got wheels, and it's got brakes. Ain't nothing wrong with it."

"It's too small," I'd protest, "and all the other kids ride cool bikes with banana seats and butterfly handlebars."

"I'll see about getting you some new handlebars, and you can get a long seat if you want to put it on there yourself, *but that bike is fine.*"

So to this day, if you were to ask my mom, my sister, and me what we remember most about Dad, we'd smile and say in unison: "The man was *cheap*."

I never got a Schwinn Sting-Ray, but Dad did teach me a great deal about basketball. When I was in the third grade, he bought me my first new ball, and I carried it with me all the time. Not too long after that, he put up a basketball goal so I could practice shooting.

I didn't have a lot of natural ability—I tried my best to put the ball through the net, but ten feet was just too high. I had to launch the ball more like a shot put than a basketball.

My frustration could have easily defeated me, but my dad understood. To make sure I wouldn't get discouraged and give up, he lowered the basket to about seven feet. Every couple of months he'd raise it a little. Eventually, the hoop was eight feet from the ground, then nine, and finally, when he knew I was strong enough, he moved it to the regulation ten feet.

We've all heard the saying "Practice makes perfect." Well, it might not make perfect, but as my dad said to me over and over again, "Practice makes for *improvement*." He found ways to build my confidence while teaching me the fundamentals of the game, strengthening my body for competitive play, and keeping me challenged enough that I still had to work hard to improve.

When I first started playing competitively on a team and doing well, I'd come home after the games and tell my father how many points I'd scored. Dad, in an effort to keep me from getting too cocky, would interrupt me with an important message: "Don't you ever forget that there's somebody else out there who's working harder, who's just as tall, and probably better than you. Even though you're scoring a lot of points and your team might be winning, you probably haven't met a worthy opponent, so you'd better humble yourself and continue to work hard."

But there was also another factor that figured into my

father's critique of my abilities . . . he used to brag about how good *he* was at everything. He'd tell me over and over that he was a great basketball player, and then he'd take me out on the court to show me what he meant.

He'd often challenge me to play a game called HORSE. It's a game that requires you to match the other player's shot. For example, if I made a hook shot with my right hand off the backboard, then my dad would have to make a hook shot with his right hand off the backboard from the same distance. If he missed the shot, he'd be given the letter "H." For each shot a player misses, another letter is added until HORSE is spelled and the game is over. The object is to make your shots difficult ones, knowing that your opponent probably won't match them.

"You can't just shoot with your right hand," Dad would instruct. "You've got to work on your left hand." My dad knew I had a hard time making shots with my left hand, so he'd demonstrate how well he could shoot with either hand—and chalk up another victory.

The first few years we played, he always won. But by the time I was 13, I began *letting* him win. I did that for three years until finally, when I was 16, I had to say to him, "Okay, you still think you can beat me? I need to go ahead and whip you."

And I did.

▲ ▲ ▲

Initially, I didn't have a strong desire to play basketball as part of a team—but if you're tall, people expect you to. Today, I joke in my speeches, "I wonder why no one asked me to be a jockey."

My first exposure to organized basketball was with the East Madison YMCA. One day my cousin Peanut came by with the Y's coach, Steve Ewing. He liked my height and my attitude, so he put me on the team. It was a new experience for me, since up to that point all I'd done was shoot hoops at school and at home.

When I was put in my very first game, I had to rely on Peanut's directions, because I still didn't know all the rules. When we were on defense, Peanut urged, "Stay in the lane, Keith. Put your hands up on defense." I nodded and did exactly as he said.

Then I went down to the other end of the court where we were on offense. Once again I stood in the middle of the lane. But this time the referee blew his whistle and yelled, "Three seconds!" pointing an accusing finger my way.

"Keith, you can't stand in the lane!" Peanut explained.

"But you just told me to."

"That was on *defense.* Now you're on *offense.* You only have three seconds to stay in the painted area. You have to move in and out."

Figuring out the rules on the fly was frustrating, but it was exciting to be a part of a team. After that first experience, I played for several different teams because my dad used to say, "If you really want to be good, you have to play all the time." So I became a member of the Garfield Recreational team, my school's team, and the Catholic Youth Organization's (CYO) team.

That team was a very good one—we won the CYO City Tournament when I was 14, so we were invited to play for the state championship. I hurt my ankle in the first half of that game and had to play the second half with it taped up, but we won.

When we got back to town, I had my ankle x-rayed. To my amazement, the doctor told me it was broken. The local newspaper got hold of this tidbit and wrote a story with the headline "Harrell Plays Second Half on Broken Ankle." (Actually, I played better on a broken ankle than I did with two good ones.)

And what was Dad's response to the article? He played it

down, of course—I was starting to get used to it. I can see now that this was his way of motivating me to always try harder.

▲ ▲ ▲

When I think of the phrase "Practice makes for improvement," I always think about the importance of setting goals. Early on, my dad helped me set small, reachable goals as a defensive move to fend off an attitude of frustration—it may be the most important thing he taught me. As I reached those goals, he'd help me set new ones.

So when I made the transition from shooting hoops with my friends to playing basketball on a team, it seemed natural to start watching college and professional games to increase my understanding of the sport. It was there that I found my first basketball heroes, who became my role models. I watched, listened, and read all I could about them—I wanted to be like them.

My first year I studied Jerry West of the Los Angeles Lakers, because we were about the same height. Mimicking his moves gave me confidence and showed me how to play without feeling clumsy and awkward.

I also set daily goals that were designed to allow me to reach my yearly goals. I'd continually say to myself, "By this time next year I'll be shooting from this far out, jumping this high, running this many miles, shooting this number of baskets, scoring this number of points."

The following year I read about Wilt Chamberlain, who is still the only player to have scored 100 points in an NBA game. Chamberlain's story interested me because he not only set goals for the year, but for multiple years in the future, which allowed for any setbacks he might encounter. I adopted his model in my eighth-grade year and mapped out a strategy through my senior year in high school. I set daily, monthly, and annual goals. Again, they were specific and measurable.

But most significantly, I studied "Pistol" Pete Maravich. I read that when he was developing his game, he treated his basketball like his girlfriend. He gave it a name and took it wherever he went, including the movies. I called my basketball "Diane."

"Pistol" Pete also practiced dribbling and shooting in the gym with the lights out so that he could learn to play by feel and instinct rather than by watching the ball or the hoop. I did the same thing.

He could dribble and shoot equally well with either hand, so I worked on my left-hand coordination. I'd eat, brush my teeth, and comb my hair with my left hand in order to strengthen it and become more comfortable using it.

I put a lot into basketball in my childhood and teenage years because it was a passion for me and I had a purpose. I wanted to be a high school all-American. I wanted to play basketball in college and one day get a chance to play in the NBA.

Dad always said, "If you want something bad enough, you have to work for it." I continued to spend a lot of time after school in the gym practicing. Sometimes my mom would have to call the gym to tell me to come home, because I'd stay there as long as I could.

My friend Delo Hayes and I would practice, practice, practice. I wanted to be the best basketball player I could be. I was convinced that every time I'd shoot, I'd get better. I was sure that with good coaching and hard work, there wasn't anything I couldn't do on the basketball court. And of course it didn't hurt being four or five inches taller than all my peers.

My father never came to watch me play basketball until I was in high school. It really didn't bother me because I figured if he was there, I'd put more pressure on myself. Plus, only a few of the other parents came to the games, so it was no big deal.

Dad did come to one of my Little League baseball games, though. We played near my grandmother's home, so it was convenient. We played Peanut's team, the Blue Angels.

I was 11 years old, playing left field. I was taught by my coach to back up third base just in case a ball got by the third baseman with a man on base.

Sure enough, the catcher threw a ball to tag out the man at third. He threw it wildly, the ball soaring over the third baseman's head. The runner on third took off for home plate.

I was right where I was supposed to be, backing up the third baseman. I bent down on my knee, scooped up that ball, and threw a rifle shot to home plate. It landed squarely in the catcher's mitt. He tagged the runner just before he slid in.

"You're outta there!" the ump cried.

I can still remember what happened next. It was powerful, for it had never happened before.

I heard my Dad's booming voice booming from the stands: *"That's my son! Way to throw that rock, boy!"*

▲ ▲ ▲

LESSON 4:
Perfect Practice
▲ ▲ ▲ ▲ ▲ ▲ ▲ ▲ ▲

Can you recall a time when you were so excited about learning a new skill that you planned your day in advance to make sure you maximized your practice time? I used to do that when I was learning how to play basketball. After school, my friend Delo and I would race to the gym to show each other what we'd learned since the last time we'd practiced together. Then we'd spend hours on the court jumping, shooting, dribbling, and rebounding over and over until we were exhausted. The skills we developed would have eluded us if our commitment, focus, and desire hadn't been as strong.

Anyone who's ever achieved a level of mastery in a given field knows that the best and most efficient way to get better at a task is through perfect practice—repetition, coaching, commitment, enthusiasm, and attention to detail. If there's a new skill you want to learn, be realistic about the amount of time you'll need to achieve your desired outcome, and expect some initial awkwardness or uneasiness. Take it one step at a time, recognize modest improvements, and applaud each success—regardless of how insignificant it may seem. Find a coach or a partner to practice with, and be patient with yourself. Remember, if you're having fun, then you're bound to get better.

CHAPTER 5

· · · · · · · · · · · ·

My First Paycheck

*"Lazy people don't even cook the
game they catch, but the diligent make
use of everything they find."*
— Proverbs 12:27

I was excited to be nearing my final days at Stevens Elementary School. I was really looking forward to junior high—and like most sixth-graders, I wanted to be able to dress like my friends and keep up with the fads.

But my dad was no different from many fathers whose kids felt that they were in need of the most current gadgets or clothing trends. When I'd ask him for something, his standard response was, "When I was a boy, I never had . . ." You can fill in the rest.

Toward the end of that school year, however, he'd changed his tactic. Whenever I'd say I wanted something, he'd reply, "You always want things with *my* money. If you want something, *you* need to go out and work hard for it."

One day I finally shot back, "Well, then, how can I make

my own money?"

"Get a job."

So I did. Not long after that conversation, I met a boy named Robbie who told me he had a paper route. He described what was involved, and the more I heard about it, the more I liked it . . . especially the part about getting paid!

That night at dinner, I asked my dad, "Can I have a paper route?"

"We'll see," he responded, as if he hoped I'd soon lose interest.

But I didn't forget about it—in fact, I started telling my friends that I'd gotten a job. "I'm going to be delivering newspapers," I told them.

"Where's your route?" they'd ask.

"Well, I don't have one yet, but get ready. It's just a matter of time before you see me delivering the paper to your house . . . and you'll be paying me."

Several months later I ran into Robbie again while he was out on his afternoon deliveries. This time he had great news— he was going to quit. Hearing this information, I sprinted home to talk to my father.

"Dad," I said, "I saw the guy who delivers papers around here, and he said that he's decided to quit. So a route will be open real soon and I'd like to take it. Can I?"

To my absolute delight, he said yes.

We made the necessary phone calls, and a recruiter for *The Seattle Times* came by the house to explain to my dad and me the qualifications and responsibilities necessary for the job. He'd already checked my grades to make sure I was a good student, and as the conversation progressed, the recruiter turned to my dad and said, "You know, sir, it's very important that your son be *on time, accountable,* and *reliable.*" He really emphasized those three key ideas.

My dad looked me right in the eyes and said, "Keith, this is a big commitment that you're about to make. You're not only committing to *The Seattle Times,* but you're also making a commitment to me. Do you understand?"

I swallowed hard and nodded.

"I'm not going to deliver these papers for you—I already have a job. But if this is the job that *you* want, I'm going to let you make that decision. Understand?"

Again, I nodded.

"But once you make this decision, you're going to have to stick with it. So, do you still want this paper route?"

"Yes," I replied confidently.

The recruiter produced a contract committing me to one full year. He asked me to sign it.

"This is not a month-by-month agreement," Dad clarified for me. "Once you sign this, you're in for 12 months—no quitting."

"I understand."

"And it's not just weekday afternoons," he continued. "On Sunday mornings you'll have to get up and make sure the papers are delivered by six. I figure that means you're going to have to wake up at 4 A.M. Plus, you'll have to come right home every day after school to deliver the papers."

"That's right, Keith," the recruiter chimed in. "Rain, shine, snow, or hail—people want their newspaper. They want it delivered, and they want it *dry.*"

Dad and the recruiter were doing everything they could to be sure that I had a realistic picture of what delivering papers was all about. I tried to listen to what they were saying, but the idea of having my own money was influencing my ability to consider their warnings.

At that point, the recruiter regained my attention by

explaining the connection between the work and the money. "Don't forget, Keith," he said, "if you don't deliver the paper, or if we get a complaint, 50 cents will be docked from your pay."

I was doing the math in my head, and I'd already calculated that I was going to make between $30 and $40 per month. But if four or five people complained each day, I wouldn't make anything.

That was all the incentive I needed to do the job right. I remember thinking as I signed the contract that I would not only deliver those papers faithfully, but I'd be sure to put rubber bands around them, put them behind the screen door if the customer had one, and put the papers in plastic if it was raining.

A few words from Dad gave me motivation as well: "Remember now, don't come to me with any problems about the paper route; don't complain to me about the weather. I'm not going to want to hear any of it . . . it's not my job." Then he added, "Since it's your job, that also means it's your money. I'm not going to question you about what you do with it. If you want to buy a bike or those ridiculous boots you like or those funny-looking pants everyone's wearing—it's your choice. Whatever you want to spend your money on is fine with me."

This seemed beyond my wildest dreams. For the first time in my life, I felt that I had a role in making some decisions for myself. All I had to do was work hard, and then I could pay for whatever I wanted.

The biggest challenge of having a paper route was how it interfered with my love for basketball. Because of the route, I had to run home to deliver the papers after school, and then I'd sprint to the gym—sometimes playing ball late into the night.

It made the weekends interesting as well. If I had a basketball game on Saturday, I had to make sure I could play the game and get back home early enough to deliver the afternoon paper.

Sometimes my dad would go fishing at Moses Lake for the weekend, but I had to stay home now that I had a job.

On Sundays I'd finish delivering the papers just in time to go to Sunday school. My mom always made sure that regardless of how long it took me to do my route, I'd be done in time for her to drop me off at church. Of course, you already know how I handled Sunday school from an earlier chapter—and yes, I was still skipping out on it.

I was doing a good job of delivering the papers, but I was having a tough time collecting the money. I had a little receipt book, and at the end of each month I was expected to collect what people owed. The charge for daily and Sunday delivery was only $3.50 per month, but I was amazed at how many people didn't want to pay me on time.

"Come back next week," "I didn't get my paycheck yet," "I got my check, but I haven't had time to cash it," "Come back when my mom is here," or "I'll pay you when my husband gets home."

All this hassle over a measly little $3.50.

Sometimes I got so discouraged that I wanted to give up. I didn't dare tell Dad, but eventually Mom could tell I was frustrated. "You're working so hard," she told me. "But if you want to be able to buy the things you want, then you'll have to go get your money."

"But I don't know what to do," I confessed.

"Tell these people that they can't get their paper until you get your money."

My mom taught me a valuable lesson about accounts receivable at an early age: *If you do the work, people need to pay for it.*

Collecting was more difficult than delivering, but delivering was not without its problems. Sundays were a special challenge because of the added weight of the newspaper. With the comics, extended editorials, *Parade* magazine, and an additional real-estate section, the Sunday edition could come in at 275 pages—making my load extremely heavy.

Add to the weighty papers the fact that I had to get up in the dark at four in the morning, and the picture was complete. I'd always been afraid of the dark, and it didn't help that I lived in a part of Seattle that was heavily wooded. I can still vividly recall those pitch-black mornings when I'd run through the woods in order to finish as quickly as possible. I know there were Sunday mornings when I received my papers at 4:00 and everybody had a paper by 4:30.

Over the Thanksgiving holiday that year it was especially cold, so in addition to my usual winter garb, I put on an extra pair of long johns, two sweatshirts, and a scarf. Before I left on my route, I set a glass of water outside just to see how cold it really was. By the time I returned, the water was frozen solid. It turned out to be 17 degrees that day. I considered asking for help, but Dad's words were still strong in my mind: "I don't care what the weather conditions are like: *Don't wake me up.*"

Later that winter there was another bad storm. I remember going into my parents' bedroom—not to bother my dad, but to wake up my mom. She'd told me the night before, "It's dangerous for you to be out there alone; it's too cold. I'm going to take the car out and go with you."

I was so grateful for her help that day.

During that entire year, my mother helped me twice. I hadn't asked her to help me, however, and I was sure to inform my father of this both times. Dad never said anything about it—I guess he didn't mind that she was helping, as long as he didn't have to get up, too.

I had a perfect 365-day record on that paper route. And

what were two of the greatest moments of that year? The day I got my *first* paycheck, and the day I got my *last* paycheck.

Oh, and by the way, I didn't sign up a second time.

▲ ▲ ▲

LESSON 5:
No Free Lunch
▲ ▲ ▲ ▲ ▲ ▲ ▲ ▲ ▲

The pursuit of dreams, visions, and goals comes at a cost. There is no free lunch. I now laugh every time I see an ad for some wonderful service or gift that's "absolutely free." I've had friends who'd call me up to tell me about an offer for a free vacation, cellular phone, or whatever. I'd get on the phone only to discover that the "free" vacation packages involved time-share condominiums and the "free" cell-phone deals required me to sign up for a long-term service agreement. Now my response is, "Read the fine print—there's no such thing as a 'free lunch.'" It's a lesson I remember my grandmother teaching, and my dad confirmed that for me when he allowed me to start my first job as a paper boy.

When I entered into an agreement with *The Seattle Times*, I was focused on making money; I didn't fully realize the sacrifices I'd have to make in order to obtain it. I'd made a commitment to be responsible, on time, accountable, and reliable. Work took precedence over my time, comfort, and interests. Neither my dad nor my customers cared about the weather conditions or what plans I may have had; they were depending on me to keep my word.

I joined the job force with one goal in mind: to get paid! I soon learned that there would always be obstacles in the way of achieving my goal. Even though I kept my end of the bargain, many of my customers didn't keep theirs. So collecting money became my obstacle.

There will always be obstacles in your way as you pursue your dreams and goals. There will be sacrifices and individuals and circumstances that may cause you to become discouraged. Just remember that there are no free lunches, and anything worth having is worth working for. As a result, you'll discover that the reward will be greater than a paycheck: You'll have earned the respect of those you serve!

CHAPTER 6

· · · · · · · · · · · · · · · ·

I'm Not Going to
Stutter Anymore

*"Now go, and do as I have told you.
I will help you speak well,
and I will tell you what to say."*
— Exodus 4:12

The thought of my first day of junior high had filled me
with excitement and opportunity for some time. It was
just what I wanted—a new school, new people, and new teachers: the perfect opportunity to start over.

Even though most of my former classmates went to the
same junior high, we were separated into different homerooms.
In my case, there weren't any people in my homeroom class who
knew me from my days back at Stevens Elementary School . . .
so they didn't know about my stuttering.

"Keith Harrell, would you please come to the front of the
classroom?" were the first words I heard from Mr. Brown, my
new homeroom teacher.

I was surprised by his request. *Maybe he just wants me to*

volunteer for something, I thought, as I walked to the front of the room. I decided that this was an opportune time to display my confidence to my new teacher, as well as my peers.

"Keith," he said softly, "there's been a change in your schedule. Instead of coming to homeroom, you'll need to go to speech-therapy class."

I was totally shocked. I remember trying to whisper back to him, because I didn't want the class to know what we were talking about. "Mr. Brown, there's been a mistake—I don't think I'm supposed to go there anymore. I've gotten very good at speaking. They told me I did very well in my last speech class at Stevens. I've grown out of stuttering."

I was continually getting taller, and my grandmother's words about "outgrowing it" had stuck with me. I was convinced that I didn't belong in speech therapy any longer. Plus, I'd a made a decision: *I'm not going to stutter anymore.* As far as I was concerned, the stuttering and the teasing were history.

Mr. Brown seemed to sense my new resolve. "Why don't you take this note down to the teacher. Tell him what you just told me, and have him make a recommendation."

I walked out of the classroom and headed for speech therapy. I'd made a similar journey dozens of times back at Stevens Elementary, but this time it was different—and not just because I'd changed schools. I was filled with confidence and self-assurance. "I don't stutter anymore," I visualized myself telling the speech therapist. I kept repeating out loud, "I'm not going to stutter anymore; I've grown out of it. I don't stutter anymore."

The walk took about ten minutes, since the speech-therapy room was on the other side of the school. I had total mental focus on my mission. I kept repeating my mantra—I was in a zone.

When I opened the door to walk into the class, I felt a familiar sense of nervousness wash over me. But I remembered what my therapist back at Stevens had taught me: "When you feel the adrenaline of nervousness, just tell yourself, 'I'm excited. It's controlled enthusiasm.'"

My heart started pounding and my breathing began getting shallow. That's what typically happens to me when I get excited—and that's when I start to stutter. But this time I used what I'd learned, both in speech class and over the summer. I told myself, *Okay, you're getting ready. Here comes the adrenaline, pumping you up and getting you full of enthusiasm.* I kept telling myself to just stay calm.

I walked confidently to the front of the classroom. Mr. Smith, the speech therapist, was at his desk. I handed him the note and proceeded to say, "I don't stutter anymore. I've worked hard on my speech exercises. I was told that I was going to grow out of it, and I've practiced all summer. Somebody else needs to take my seat; somebody else needs the opportunity, Mr. Smith. You probably need the space."

I pointed to the class as I spoke, since I'd noticed the moment I walked in that it was full.

Mr. Smith replied, "Keith, I am *very* proud of you."

I smiled.

"But," he continued, "I can't just dismiss you from speech therapy on your word. You do seem to have a great deal of confidence, and you're speaking very well right now, but we'll need to do an evaluation."

I guess Mr. Smith could tell that I was disappointed with what he'd said, because he didn't ask me to have a seat. Instead, he handed me a book. "I'll tell you what," he proposed. "Why don't we just evaluate you right now? Why don't you turn around and read a couple of paragraphs from today's lesson? Go ahead and read them to the class."

At that instant, I felt that all of the practice, speech lessons, and teasing came down to this *one moment*. I was going to show Mr. Smith that I could do it. I was going to show everyone that I didn't stutter anymore.

Mr. Smith turned to introduce me to the class. He let them know that I was someone just like them—someone who'd faced a challenge most of his life. I, too, was someone who'd been working very hard to improve. And I was someone who'd finally reached the point of feeling confident that I'd overcome my trial.

"Class, may I have your attention?" Mr. Smith announced. "I'd like to introduce Keith Harrell. We're going to give him a few minutes this morning to show us just how hard he's worked over the summer vacation to improve his speech." He added, "We want to *encourage* Keith."

Looking out at those students was so different from looking out at the kids in my elementary school. At Stevens, whenever it was my chance to read, they'd start snickering before I even opened my mouth. But these kids looked at me with anticipation. Their expressions told me: "Come on, Keith, we know you can do it."

I started reading, and I made sure to use every skill I'd learned—taking deep breaths, trying not to rush, pausing and stopping, making eye contact, nodding my head. I even remember walking, as my therapists at Stevens had advised me to do. I'd read a little bit, then walk to the other side of the classroom. I'd continue reading, and pace back.

I was in a rhythm. When I looked up from the page, the kids were leaning forward. *It was the perfect moment.* I was accomplishing the very thing I'd always wanted to do.

Mr. Smith had only asked me to read a couple of paragraphs, but before I knew it, I'd read the whole page. It was so wonderful that I stopped and asked Mr. Smith, "Do you mind if I finish the chapter?"

"Go right ahead," he encouraged. "You're doing so well."

When I finished, Mr. Smith stood up and said, "Keith did such a wonderful job—let's give him a round of applause."

The kids did more than clap . . . they gave me a standing ovation. I felt so excited. I thought, *I did it! Never again will people laugh at me because of the way I talk; never again will I feel that lack of breath on the inside of me—I won't be gasping for air. I actually did it!*

Mr. Smith wrote his recommendation on the slip I'd brought with me from my homeroom teacher. "I'll be sure a copy of this note is placed in your file down at the office," he said. I looked over his shoulder to see what he'd written: *Based on my observation, Keith Harrell no longer needs to be enrolled in speech therapy.*

"Keith, you're always welcome in my class," Mr. Smith smiled. "Come back anytime to read again or just to visit."

I remember walking out of his class feeling like a million bucks. Suddenly, I burst into a sprint because I wanted to get back to my first class before it ended. But as I was running, I thought of someone else I needed to share this moment with—someone even more important than my homeroom teacher. I had to share this moment with my mom.

She'd faithfully practiced with me over the summer. She'd listened to my tape recordings and had been the one constantly telling me to slow down and take a deep breath. Basically, she'd assumed the role of my speech therapist, so I just had to pass on the good news to her first.

By the time I reached the office, I was so excited and out of breath that the secretary thought an accident had occurred. "I have to call my mom—it's an emergency!" I implored.

"Is something wrong?"

"No—I just have to call my mom!"

"Okay, honey," the secretary consoled. "Come around the desk here and use my phone."

I dialed my mom's number at work and she answered, "Hello, this is Florence."

"M-m-mom, I just came from speech! I didn't want to go to speech, and I-I told myself I-I didn't have to go to speech b-because I had grown out of it. M-m-mom, I-I-I told them that. And Mr. Smith, the s-s-speech therapist, had me get up and r-r-read. He said if I read then I-I-I didn't have to go to s-speech class anymore, and . . . "

Mom interrupted, "Slow down, Keith."

"M-m-mama, I-I-I don't have t-to go to s-speech anymore. I-I-I don't stutter anymore!"

"That's wonderful news, honey! You'll have to tell me more about it when you get home."

I walked out of that office as if I were walking on a cloud. It's a feeling that I remember to this day. I actually *wanted* somebody to say something to me so I could respond. They could ask me my name, ask me directions, ask me to read—it didn't matter, because I wasn't going to stutter anymore. For the first time in my life, I felt in control of the words that came out of my mouth.

When I returned to homeroom, I didn't immediately go up to the teacher. I decided I'd play it cool. After all, the kids didn't know where I'd been. After class, I went up to him and showed him the note.

He read it, looked at me with a proud smile, and made the "okay" sign with his fingers.

I smiled back and thought, *That's right—I don't stutter anymore.*

LESSON 6:
Say It, Believe It, and Receive It!
▲ ▲ ▲ ▲ ▲ ▲ ▲ ▲ ▲

"I don't stutter anymore!" This was my dream, my aspiration, and my goal. My mother had told me that she knew that one day her little boy would be able to stand up and say his name just like all the other kids. That day came for me in the seventh grade. I didn't just say my name, I read a whole chapter of a book—out loud and in front of a classroom of my peers. Today I stand in front of thousands of men and women and proudly announce, "My name is Keith Harrell!"

Okay, I must confess that I still stutter a little on occasion. But what I learned from six years of speech therapy and many more years of my own research was that if I repeatedly affirmed the thing I wanted the most—in this situation, not to stutter—then I could convince my subconscious mind that my ambition was a reality!

Each of us has the same ability to overcome a challenge or defeat a doubt. We can conquer our uncertainties by positively proclaiming what we want in our lives. We can override our "internal computers" and reprogram our subconscious minds.

The first step is to say it: Say it out loud, say it to others, write it, and post it on notes that you'll see throughout the day. Second, you must believe it. I always believed that one day I wouldn't stutter; I believed it with all my heart. It's amazing how attitude and behavior follow the desires of the heart. And last, receive it. Allow yourself to visualize the end—see yourself with the job you want, or the vacation you've dreamed of, or reaching the academic goal you've been working toward. When you continually declare to yourself and others those things that you desire, then your outlook, attitude, and behavior will change to support your newly created belief.

So say it, believe it, and receive it! What's keeping you from obtaining your goals and triumphing over the obstacles in your life? What you need to do is affirm the things you want and make your dreams a reality!

CHAPTER 7

· · · · · · · · · · · · · · ·

Dreams with Deadlines

*"My child, don't lose sight of good
planning and insight. Hang on to them,
for they fill you with life and bring
you honor and respect."*
— Proverbs 3:21–22

As a member of the junior high basketball team, I started to become a popular guy around campus. But because of all the unwanted attention I'd received as a result of my height and my stuttering, I was still extremely reserved. Being tall had turned out to be a great advantage when it came to playing ball, and I'd conquered my stuttering after years of hard work—but I wasn't sure how to overcome my shyness. It wasn't until around the eighth grade that I began to get a handle on this issue, and in part, I have the CYO State Championship and my broken ankle to thank for that.

Due to my injury, I had to have my leg in a cast. Worse, I couldn't put any weight on it. Imagine a 6'4" eighth-grader limping on crutches that were taller than most of the kids, and even some of the teachers. Needless to say, I felt awkward and self-conscious.

Trying to maneuver to class between periods was challenging, and to make matters more difficult, I had to deal with a bunch of unsympathetic adolescent guys. They'd rib me and run me down in the halls, calling out, "Get out of my way, cripple! Move, man, move!"

But the girls were different. They'd ask, "Can I carry your books, Keith?" "Are you going to be okay?" " How did it happen?" "Oh, wow, is it painful?" " How long do you have to wear the cast?" "What do you do if it itches?" and best of all, "Can I sign it?"

I declared, "The only people who'll be signing my cast are *girls*. And if you want to sign it, you have to write down your phone number because I've got to let everyone know how my ankle is doing. Don't put your number down unless you're giving me permission to call you."

A competition of sorts ensued. "Oh, Janet has her name and number on your cast? Let me put mine on it, too. I'm going to put mine in pink," one girl cooed.

Another piped up, "I'm going to put circles around mine."

The girls debated over how they were going to write their names and how they were going to color-coordinate my cast. It became a showpiece.

I took good care of that cast because of all it was affording me—I'd managed to get every phone number I wanted during the months it took for the fracture to heal. So I'd hang my leg outside the shower to keep the cast dry, and I'd make sure that it had all kinds of plastic and tape around it to protect it from the rain.

I also began to rethink the way I dressed. I'd always admired my dad's wardrobe—he was a nice dresser. He liked pinstripes and sharkskin suits, was meticulous about his shoes (he paid my sister, Toni, to keep them polished), and I noticed that he always got his shirts starched.

So I asked Mom if I could get some of my shirts starched, too. I took all the money I'd saved from my paper route and bought some high-collared shirts and nice jeans. All we wore back then were Levi 501's—and to look good, they had to have the right cuff, a nice line running down the center of each leg, and they had to be *starched*.

Not only was I going through a can of starch every four days on my jeans, but now I was getting my shirts laundered with heavy starch. I'd cut a slit in the leg of my pants to fit over my cast, so there I was with a pair of stiff jeans, my starched shirt, and a matching sock on my good leg.

Some of the guys noticed my new look, and I got a nickname: "Hey, King Starch, what's going on?"

Yes, I was coming out of my shyness shell. "Today it's going to be a fashion show," I'd tell myself. "What shirt should I wear with my starched jeans today?" Before my broken ankle, I didn't want to draw any attention to myself; now I was dressing to impress and calling girls on the phone.

It was around this same time that I began to take kung fu lessons with my friend LeeRoy Clayton, Jr. Bruce Lee had been co-starring in a television show called *The Green Hornet,* and, as a result, everybody in my crowd was really into martial arts. We'd walk around the neighborhood kicking our feet high in the air at imaginary villains.

"Hey, I know a guy who'll teach us kung fu for real," LeeRoy told me one day. "Are you interested?"

"Sure," I replied.

Initially, I wanted to learn kung fu so that I'd be able to defend myself. I also thought it was going to be fun. I was wrong. It didn't take long before I was dreading going to lessons because I knew I'd be in for a two-and-a-half-hour period of sweat and hard work. Our instructor, Master Mar, would lead us through the various stances, and we'd practice our breathing. Then we'd do hand and arm exercises, which were followed by sit-ups, crunches, kicks, and squats. I learned how to eat properly and stay alert. Basically, I was being conditioned both physically and mentally.

This all sounds so positive in retrospect, but at the time, *I hated it.* I wanted to learn how to fight so that I'd be able to protect myself if I had to—just like Bruce Lee did on television. But to my disappointment, we didn't get to spar much in our classes. What I really learned from Master Mar was respect for myself and others. Master Mar taught us discipline, commitment, and the importance of taking care of our bodies. Consequently, I developed mental toughness and endurance. I often look back and realize that those are the qualities that have given me an edge when life's been rough.

I now see that kung fu reinforced the importance of several life lessons, such as respecting my peers, being responsible, working hard, and achieving mastery of mind over body. As a result of kung fu, I matured.

Kung fu also gave me an insight into human behavior. For example, it provided me with an awareness of *why* people tease others. I saw that people had picked on me because of weakness on their part; as a result, I was able to look at the situation differently because I understood that it was their low self-esteem that caused them to ridicule me. I decided to show respect for these people—even though I now knew several different ways to slap them upside the head if I wanted to.

Seriously, though, I began to see people in a different way. I knew who *I* was, so I didn't need to worry about what others said. And when someone did say something that bothered me, I learned to use that negative comment as positive motivation to reach my goals.

My friend Delo Hayes provided me with the perfect opportunity to put this method into practice. Delo and I were extremely competitive. He was much shorter than I was, so on the basketball team he played guard while I always played center. Delo had two older twin brothers who were fairly good basketball players, and he'd learned a lot about "trash talking" from them. He used their insults pretty regularly on me.

Delo and I played a lot of one-on-one together because the older guys wouldn't let us play with them. We played so much that we'd be the last two people at the gym almost every night—they'd have to turn out the lights to get us to leave.

We had great games that were pretty evenly balanced: He'd win some and I'd win some. But I recall one night in particular when I lost because of a lucky fade-away shot Delo made in desperation at the end of the game. As we walked home from the gym with his brothers, he began to talk trash.

"Can you believe I beat this guy tonight?" he blurted out to his siblings. They laughed in response, and then he turned to me. "How tall are you, 6'4"?"

I didn't answer. Delo knew how tall I was.

"I'm only 5'5"!" he howled.

I knew where this was going.

"How can you let a little guy like me beat a big guy like you?" he mocked.

By now all his brothers were getting into it, too. "Man, you're so sorry," they taunted. "You ought to be playing with the girls. You ought to give up on basketball. How could you let him beat you?"

"Yeah, how could you get beat so badly by a little guy like

me?" Delo chimed in.

They went on and on the entire walk home.

I'd had enough. *"You will never beat me again for the rest of your life!"* I snapped at Delo.

When I got home, I mentioned it to my dad.

"If you're going to say things like that, it's very important that you back them up," Dad replied.

"How?" I asked.

"Well, I'm talking about the importance of setting goals. Take Cassius Clay, for example." (This was before the boxer had changed his name to Muhammad Ali.) "He backs up his words with his actions."

I was a big fan of Clay. Whenever he had a fight, I'd listen to it on the radio. I remember there had been several times when I had to go to bed before the fight was over. But it didn't matter, because it was usually obvious that he'd won long before the last round.

"All good athletes set goals," Dad continued, "then they do the extra work necessary to accomplish them. The important thing is to set the goal, have a plan, and work toward that goal. Understand?"

I appreciated what my father said, and the concept of setting goals became integral in my life. I never told Delo, but that night I set a goal that I'd work a little harder every time I went to the gym so that the next time we played I would be mentally and physically prepared. I was *not* going to let him beat me again.

That year, the school district announced that all current eighth-grade students would be going to high school to start off as freshman in the fall. I was bummed out about it because I was looking forward to being the big shot ninth-grader on the junior high campus, and now I'd be missing out on that whole experience. But I made the best of it.

At the end of eighth grade, I signed all of my friends' year books: *1974 Garfield High School State Champs. All-American, averaging over 25 points and 18 rebounds per game—Keith Harrell, 6 feet, 9 inches.*

"Dude, what you doin' writing that?" my classmates responded in disbelief.

"Well, you said you wanted me to write something positive," I'd reply. "That's my goal statement. I'm writing it because all great athletes set goals and start telling people what they're going to do. It helps them achieve."

"How do you know Garfield's going to win the state championship?" they'd ask. "How do you know you're going to be an all-American?"

I'd always respond the same way: "I have 365 days times four years to make it happen. I've been reading books about Pete Maravich, Jerry West, and Wilt Chamberlain, and I'm ready to work hard. I'm going to improve in some way every day, so I know nobody's going to be able to keep me from achieving my dream."

Back then, I merely thought of my bold statement as analogous to trash-talking. I figured that since I didn't have an opportunity to be the big man on campus as a ninth grader, in 1974, my senior year of high school, I'd be an all-American. Writing that goal statement motivated me. What I was doing was stating an affirmation and claiming the victory: I told everyone that this was what I was going to do. We'd be state champs—I just knew it.

My first experience with setting goals made a tremendous difference in building my confidence. And I have Delo and his "trash-talking" brothers to thank.

▲ ▲ ▲

LESSON 7:
Turning Points into Learning Points
▲ ▲ ▲ ▲ ▲ ▲ ▲ ▲ ▲

We all have turning points in our lives—incidents or events that cause us to refocus and change directions. Two major turning points occurred for me in the eighth grade: I broke my ankle, which helped me overcome my shyness; and my friend Delo beat me on the basketball court, which helped me understand the importance of setting goals.

Written goal statements, commonly known as *vision* or *mission statements,* enable a person to focus on desired outcomes. Each time I look at one of my written goal statements, I ask myself if my actions are bringing me closer to my goals. If they aren't, I refocus my attention.

Take the time to develop goals for yourself, and know that all things are possible for those who believe. You'll gain confidence in your ability to accomplish your goal as you replace fear and doubt with a clear vision, solid goals, and planned objectives.

So the next time you come to a turning point in your life and you're standing at a crossroads, ask yourself: "How can I make this a learning point?" There are unlimited possibilities awaiting you!

CHAPTER 8

. . . .

I'll See You Later, Dad

"The testing of your faith
produces endurance."
— James 1:3

January 1969 wasn't just another month in a typically cold, rainy Seattle winter. Another kind of storm had been brewing inside my home for years, and it was all about to come to a head—leaving me filled with confusion, guilt, shame, and despair for years to come. Even though it happens to hundreds of families each day, no facts or statistics could make it any easier for me to accept. That winter, my father and mother split up.

One day I came home from playing basketball at the gym to find my dad in my parents' bedroom packing his suitcase. Instinctively, I knew something was wrong.

"Keith," he said, "we need to talk."

I reluctantly walked into the room.

"I've got to leave," he said quietly.

I felt as if I'd been hit with a stun gun.

"You know your mother and I haven't gotten along in years.

I'm going to live somewhere else. We're getting a divorce."

I didn't know what to say. So many thoughts were swirling through my mind, but I couldn't think of any response to what I'd just been told. I blurted out, "Can you give me a ride?"

"Where do you want to go?" my father asked.

"Can you drop me off at the gym?"

I'd just *come* from the gym, but I didn't know how else to pierce the awkward and painful silence that now filled the room. Of course, what I really wanted to ask him was: "Why do you have to leave? Are you sure you're doing the right thing? Can't you and Mom find a way to work it out? Can't you give it another try?"

▲ ▲ ▲

My mother married my father right after she graduated from high school. Personally, I couldn't remember a time when they didn't argue or fight. Dad was nearly six years mom's senior and ran a strict household—he lived by one set of rules and expected her to live by another. My mother, an outgoing and independent woman, wouldn't abide by his double standard. As Mom often said, "We agreed to disagree."

I remember staying out late with my mom and her girlfriends on weekend nights. When we got home, Dad would sometimes be waiting for us. There wouldn't be any confrontation right away, but after I went to bed, it would start.

I'd hear the loud and frightening noise coming from their bedroom like a thunderstorm. There would be the sound of objects being thrown and breaking, then an audible eruption of physical violence as my parents struggled with each other. It was usually at this point that my sister, Toni, would run into their room and do her best to break it up.

My sister and I were very different in how we handled our parents' fighting. As soon as I heard the arguments begin, I'd become frozen with fear. Toni, a year-and-a-half older than I, would take a very aggressive, proactive approach, doing whatever she could to get in the middle of the disagreement and quiet things down. It makes perfect sense that Toni became a police officer—she grew up to make a living doing what she learned as a child.

"You two stop fighting!" Toni would plead and scream.

That rarely helped, so next she'd run downstairs and call our grandmother, who lived right around the corner. Grandma would drive over in her car and knock on the door, and my parents would stop arguing as soon as they heard someone at the door.

Grandma would walk in, scolding, "What's going on here? You two ought to be ashamed of yourselves!"

She had a powerful and palpable presence. Once she entered the room, my dad would immediately cease his yelling, quietly walk back to the bedroom, and go to sleep.

Meanwhile, I'd remain completely paralyzed in my bedroom. I was terrified of what I was hearing, and I wanted no part of it. I'd have conversations with myself in which I'd pretend to speak to my parents. I'd say things like: "Dad, you shouldn't be hitting Mom," or "Mom, you shouldn't stay out so late."

But I couldn't actually verbalize those words to either of them, and I *never* left my bed. I knew I didn't want to see what was going on—hearing it was bad enough. (Looking back, I realize that my lingering fear of the dark had to do, at least in part, with the trauma of domestic violence, because the fights at my house always erupted at night.)

The disputes seemed to always center on the fact that Mom came home late or was keeping Toni and me out too late. I couldn't understand why Mom wouldn't change. I didn't know it then, but my father's nasty temper and control issues were about *him,* not about my mom. And it wasn't until years later, during a holiday meal shared with my mom and sister, that I learned an important piece of information.

"Do you remember how angry your dad used to get about us coming in late?" my mom asked.

"I sure do," I replied.

"Well, did you know that your dad would yell at me for being late when he'd only gotten home *five minutes earlier?*"

"What?" I responded in disbelief.

"That's right," Mom continued. "He wanted us home—he wanted *me* home. But I said to myself, 'Why should I stay home? He's never home, so why should I have to wait here? I'm going out with my friends.'"

As I sat listening to her, all I could think about was how much I hated the fighting. Violence is rarely warranted, but in the case of domestic disputes, it's never an acceptable option.

▲ ▲ ▲

I didn't have much to say as my dad drove me to the gym that night. I kept telling myself I was going to try to be understanding. I knew I didn't want my parents to get a divorce, but I also didn't want them to continue fighting. I decided I was going to do my best to handle the situation. Of course, I still had a lot of unresolved feelings, but time would have to help me sort them out.

When we arrived at the front of the gym, I opened the car door and got out. Turning around, I said the only words that came to mind: "I'll see you later, Dad."

▲ ▲ ▲
LESSON 8:
Life's Inescapable Fact:
Problems, Pain, and Disappointment
▲ ▲ ▲ ▲ ▲ ▲ ▲ ▲ ▲

Problems, pain, and disappointment. It's an inescapable fact of life. Whether a national tragedy—like the September 11, 2001, terrorist act against America; or a personal trauma—like the loss of a loved one or getting laid off from a job, some situations in life leave us forever changed. How we choose to cope will cause us to either get bitter or better.

The trauma of living through my parents' volatile marriage and their subsequent divorce left me devastated. Intellectually, I knew it was best for them not to live together, but emotionally it was hard to handle. Explaining my dad's absence from the home was embarrassing, and my denial dragged on because I desperately wanted to believe that he'd be returning soon. Like most children whose parents divorce, my mom and dad's inability to work through their marital difficulties had a tremendous impact on me.

My reactions ran the normal gamut—shock, disappointment, anxiety, guilt, pain, and confusion. If you've ever suffered a major loss, you know what I'm talking about. And if you haven't endured one yet, just live a little longer and you will. It's part of the human experience.

While time eventually dulls acute emotional pain, immediate comfort and strength can be found in God. To anyone reading these words who's suffered a loss and may still be struggling to cope with the effects, I'd like to leave you with the following blessing:

The Lord bless you and keep you
the Lord make his face shine upon you
and be gracious to you;
the Lord turn his face toward you
and give you peace.
— Numbers 6:24–26

In your times of greatest need, just call on God. He will see you through.

CHAPTER 9

● ● ● ● ● ● ● ● ● ● ● ● ●

Smooth As Silk

*"Every good and perfect gift
is from above."*
— James 1:17

With life at home topsy-turvy, I became all the more focused on basketball. I was thankful that my dad had instilled in me the importance of setting goals and working hard to achieve them, and I was very committed to playing ball under the purple-and-white banner of Garfield High School. My ambition was to make the varsity team as a freshman.

I can remember tryouts that year as if they were yesterday. All of us guys were down in the locker room putting on our sweatpants and Converse shoes . . . but as I laced up my high-top Chuck Taylors, I was also preparing mentally. *I'm going to make the varsity team,* I told myself. I gave an extra tug to my floppy socks—the kind worn by Pete Maravich—and thought, *I can do this if I try hard enough.*

I closed my locker, took a deep breath, and walked over to the gymnasium. Actually, there were two gyms—one for varsity tryouts and the other for junior varsity and sophomore tryouts. I didn't hesitate for an instant; I knew which door to walk through. But no sooner had I crossed the threshold than the varsity coach came over to me.

"Son, you need to go over there," he said, pointing to the door that led to the other gym.

I momentarily froze. Since I'd always respected authority, I did as I was told. I remember hoping as I walked out that they were having varsity tryouts in both gyms. But it wasn't the case.

I was so disappointed. I kept thinking, *If I could just show you that I have the skills and the right attitude to make the team, you'd take me—even if I am just a freshman.*

Despite that initial letdown, trying out for the junior varsity (J.V.) team ended up being a very positive experience. I made it, and I even got to start. Another good thing about playing on the J.V. team was that our games were right before the varsity games. So after we finished, I'd run to the locker room, shower, dress, run back to the gym, and be seated in the front row in time to watch the other team do layups.

I'd sit there and watch the game, filled with anticipation for the day that I'd be out there in a varsity uniform of my own. When that time came, I wouldn't just play—I vowed that I'd *make an impact* and help my team win.

▲ ▲ ▲

Basketball tryouts were held the same way the following year. Again, there I was in the locker room, tieing the laces on my high-tops and adjusting my floppy socks, totally focused on making the varsity squad. Actually, there was one difference . . . this year I'd set my goals even higher. Not only would I *make* the varsity team, I'd also *start*.

I'd spent the entire summer practicing, and I was ready. And this time when I walked into the varsity gym, the coach allowed me to stay.

I had a good tryout—Coach was pleased with what he saw, so I made the varsity team as a sophomore. And I was *starting*.

Imagine my surprise when I discovered that the local newspaper was running a story on me and another player, Fred Thompson (a sophomore and starting varsity player at Franklin High School), that said we were going to have a "tremendous impact" on our respective teams. The article favored Garfield to win the Metro Conference that year, predicting that we'd take our division along the way. There were high expectations for my performance, too. That's why the first three games of my varsity career were so startling.

Our first game was at home. To my amazement, I saw my dad walk into the gym while we were warming up. It was one of the first times he'd ever come to one of my basketball games, and he couldn't have picked a better one—the whole school was pumped up for the start of a great season, especially since Garfield was expected to win it all.

Unfortunately, it didn't go as planned. We lost our first game, and I scored only five points. It was a very disappointing five points because I'd been touted as the "super-sophomore" who was supposed to lead the team to victory. But for whatever reason, the game didn't flow like I thought it would.

I tried to brush it off. Three days later we'd have another opportunity—a Friday-night home game. We concluded that we'd lost the opener due to first-game jitters, and I remember thinking, *We have a great team. We'll be okay.*

To everyone's surprise, we lost our second game, too. And again, I scored only five points. Needless to say, I was beginning to worry: *What's going on? Why is this happening? I need to regroup.* I continued to talk myself back into the proper focus. *Our third game is still at home. We'll make it up there.*

But we didn't get back on track. Instead, we lost a third time, and the "super sophomore" scored just seven points.

After that loss, Dad came by the house for the sole purpose of talking to me about basketball. "You seem to be out there running an offense," he said to me, "but you're not looking for your shots—you don't see the opportunity to score. Take your man to the basket."

So when the fourth game came around, I remembered my father's advice: "Offense is designed to get you a shot. When you have the ball, the first thing you ought to look for is the opportunity to score. Second, look to pass."

His words changed my whole outlook. As a result, we won our fourth game, and I scored 18 points.

From then on, I always looked to score first and pass second. We finished our season strong, and we beat all the teams we were supposed to. Even though we didn't win the division or the city championship, it was still a good year because we turned it around—thanks to Dad's suggestion and the excellent play of my teammates. I even ended up being selected for the Second Team All-City.

▲ ▲ ▲

There were high hopes for the Garfield basketball team my junior year. We had a couple of new players join the team: Larry Griffin, one of the best high school players I'd ever seen, had transferred from Queen Ann High; and Leon Johnson had come up from J.V. With the help of Philip Thorton and another outstanding guard named JoJo Rodriguez, the starting five were determined to win it all.

I continued to model my play after the style of great basketball players. I was about 6'6" that year, so I wanted to choose a player who was similar to me in height and technique. Since one of my dreams from childhood was to someday play for the legendary UCLA coach, John Wooden, it seemed natural that I'd emulate someone on his team.

I'd watched the Bruins win championship after championship during their glory years with the help of Keith Wilkes. Wilkes had a style that was so easy and effortless that he was nicknamed "Silk"—as in "Smooth As Silk." (Even though Keith Wilkes later changed his name to Jamal Wilkes, he was always known as "Silk.") He was exactly the kind of player I wanted to be, so I patterned my game after him and took on the same moniker.

My friends and family all picked up on it. Some called me "Smooth," but almost everyone called me "Silk." When I started driving, my license plate even said "Silk." A friend carved a sign in wood shop that read "Smooth As Silk," which I hung up right by our front door at home. A picture of it even ended up in the school yearbook.

But it wasn't just an attitude—my new name influenced my manner on the court as well. If there was a pressure-filled moment with the crowd going wild, I'd just make sure I was as cool as could be. It was all about making every move look seamless, and avoiding any show of emotion or excitement.

During one summer-league game against our archrivals, the Franklin High Quakers, I remember running the ball from one end of the court to the other. They had a full press on me, but I dribbled around two people, bounced the ball between my legs and around my back, spun around, crossed over to the foul line, and came up on one of their defenders. He tried to steal the ball from me, but I took it around my back. As I did, I noticed my teammate Larry Griffin cutting toward the basket. While looking the other way, I effortlessly threw the ball underneath the defender's arm, right into Larry's waiting hands. He leaped way above the rim and dropped it down for an easy basket.

It was a wild scene—the crowd started throwing things into the air, clapping, whooping, and hollering. They hadn't seen a play like that in a long time. Everyone went crazy—that is, everyone except me. I just ran down the court as if nothing had happened, because that's how someone smooth behaved. I made it look like that play happened all the time.

Yes, on the outside I was as smooth as silk. But I must admit that on the inside, I found myself thinking, *Man, I wish I had that play on film!* The more I thought about it, the more it amazed me.

The first game of the regular season was at home against Shorecrest High School. I was still adhering to my dad's counsel about "looking to score," and the outcome was decidedly different from my first game as a sophomore. We won—and I scored *32 points.*

We were unstoppable! I honestly believe the difference was that we'd set goals: We were going to win the division, and we were going to be city champs. Garfield hadn't won a city championship in more than ten years, so there was a lot of hype about it.

Our victorious season took us all the way to the city championship game, which was played at the Seattle Center Coliseum. It was us against Roosevelt High School. They had an all-star center named James Edwards who was awesome; he went on to play 18 years in the NBA, including two championship seasons with the Detroit Pistons and one with the Chicago Bulls. Edwards's team had beaten us during the regular season, and here we were—matched up again for the championship.

I was so psyched about this game. It was unbelievable—all my life I'd wanted an all-city letterman's jacket, and now I had the opportunity to earn one. All we had to do was win.

The game didn't start out very well for me. It didn't help that Roosevelt double-teamed me most of the time, but mostly I think I was just too excited. I didn't score much, but I did pull down 18 rebounds.

Fortunately, the rest of the team made up for my struggles. Our center, Marvin McWilliams, did an excellent job of containing James Edwards, so the outcome of the game went in our favor. We won the city championship.

The entire community came out and supported us on that incredibly festive and raucous occasion. The team had a chartered bus that took us to and from the Coliseum, and on the way back to our school, the bus broke down. We were so excited about winning that we didn't even mind walking the two or three miles back to Garfield.

Since we won the city championship, we went on to play in the state tournament. We were all pleasantly surprised, because we hadn't set a goal that went that far—we'd been singularly focused on winning the city championship. As a consequence, we didn't really understand anything about the regional playoffs or the state championship.

The Triple-A High School State Championship Tournament was held on the campus of the University of Washington at Hec Edmundson Pavilion. We won the first game, which sent us to the semifinals. Our opponents? Good old Roosevelt High and their star, James Edwards. We had to beat them again if we wanted to advance to the state finals.

The first half of the game went our way. We were doing a pretty good of keeping Edwards's damage to a minimum, so things were looking up. However, something must have happened in the Roosevelt locker room at halftime, because after that, they were unstoppable.

It was as if a different team had taken the court. To make matters worse, we began making some critical mistakes leading to turnovers that really hurt us. I wasn't playing up to my potential . . . and it didn't end well.

We lost, and I felt it was due to my poor efforts. My mother and sister were graduates of Roosevelt High School, so this had been more than a game against a crosstown rival; it was the rival school in my own household. It was a wake-up call for our team because it helped us see that we needed to set goals beyond the city championship.

I felt so personally responsible for our loss that I didn't even want to ride the bus back to the school—I felt unworthy. The coach called out for me, "Keith, let's go! We're about to leave."

"That's okay," I responded. "I think I'll just walk home."

Coach shrugged his shoulders, got on the bus, and it drove off. I lived about five miles away, so it gave me plenty of time to think. I had my basketball with me (I still carried that ball *everywhere*), so I walked, dribbled, and did lots of thinking.

One of my sister's girlfriends drove by in her car. She stopped, rolled down her window, and called out, "It's pretty cold out there."

"Yeah," I mumbled.

"Do you want a ride?"

"No, I'll just walk," I replied, bouncing my ball ahead of me.

Before long I was standing in front of my house. Something inside of me wasn't quite ready to go inside, so I kept walking. I must have walked six miles that night because I ended up at a neighborhood gym that stayed open late. I was acquainted with some of the guys who played there regularly, and I knew that on Friday nights they'd often be there until two or three in the morning.

I arrived around 11 P.M., and sure enough, the guys were there. They'd been listening to our game on the radio, so they knew what had happened. Fortunately, they were just about to begin a new game.

"You want to play?" one of the guys asked.

"That's why I'm here."

I came down the court and hit nothing but net, shot after shot. I thought to myself, *Why couldn't this have happened a few hours ago?* I couldn't hit a thing during the game, but now my jump shot was coming back to me. Getting my game back was a relief, and making baskets helped me to shake off the loss and refocus.

So that's what I did. That night, I made a commitment to myself that if I ever had another opportunity to play in a game where I could make a difference, I'd do whatever I could to help the team win.

That night in the gym, we played a game of "first one to 15 wins." I remember catching the ball from the top of the key (right above the free-throw circle), dribbling through my legs, spinning with two men guarding me, and releasing the ball off my fingers. As the ball flew through the air, I turned away and yelled, "Game over!" I heard the ball *swoosh* through the net, and someone on the sidelines remark, "Smooth as silk."

LESSON 9:
It's Not the Destination, It's the Journey
▲ ▲ ▲ ▲ ▲ ▲ ▲ ▲ ▲

In a time when others are flying the friendly skies, my dad still drives everywhere. He plans his trips, carefully detailing each leg of the journey. One day I asked him why. His response was simple: "It's not the destination, son, it's the journey. If you fly through life, you'll miss so much along the way."

The importance of the journey, or how we get to the place we're going—that's what I learned in this chapter of my life. Certainly you must have a vision (the destination), but the events that occur along the way are what shape a life.

When I left junior high, I had one goal, one destination—to be a starter on my championship high school basketball team. I eventually reached that goal, but it was the defeat in my junior year that made me truly reflect on the journey. It dawned on me that getting the title and the trophy was not the real reward; it was the season-long experience of being with guys who played well as a team, improved together, and celebrated each others' strengths. The destination remained the same—how I got there became the critical point.

All along my journey, I've found that modeling someone else is a great tool for enhancing performance. By modeling great basketball players such as Keith Wilkes, Wilt Chamberlain, and "Pistol" Pete Maravich, I was able to improve my basketball skills. It's a practice that's suited me well in business, too. I joined the National Speakers Association because I wanted to have access to the masters of the profession and learn from them. Zig Ziglar, Nido Qubein,

Les Brown, Thelma Wells, Larry Winget, and Hattie Hill are just a few who gave me insights on how to build my business, develop strategies, and overcome obstacles. Most important, I've modeled myself on my pastor and other men of God in order to strengthen my Christian walk.

As you journey toward your destination, take time to look at those who have succeeded before you in your field. If your goal is to be a good husband or wife, model after couples who have overcome some challenges and grown closer over the years. Talk to people in your situation. Assess the roadblocks and detours, and see what opportunities can come from the experience. But most of all, take time to enjoy life, and get pleasure from the little blessings that come your way.

Never forget your destination. However, I can tell you from experience that once you get there, it won't be the achievement you remember—it will be the journey.

CHAPTER 10

Persist Until I Win

*"A wise youth works hard all summer;
a youth who sleeps away the
hour of opportunity brings shame."*
— Proverbs 10:5

Whenever my team lost a game, I immediately found a way to analyze my own performance. I wanted to change what wasn't working and do what I needed to in order to improve, whether it was coming home and doing push-ups or sit-ups or going to the gym to work on specific moves that needed development.

The summer before my senior year, I was captain of our summer-league team. I worked so hard because of the commitment I'd made the season before, when we lost the game in the state semifinals. I dedicated every day of my life to doing something that would help the basketball team and to improving my skills. We weren't coming up short *this* year.

In addition to the summer league, I began going to the Rotary Boys' Club to work on my game. Every morning I'd get up at six, ride my bike more than five miles to the gym, and stay there all day. Some nights I closed up the place after ten. Lindsey Stuart was the director of the club, and I remember how fortunate I felt when he actually gave me a key of my own. It was a big deal for him to trust a teenager with that kind of responsibility, and I sometimes wonder where he is now and if he knows that he really made a positive difference in my life.

Not only did Lindsey stress the importance of physical discipline, but he also emphasized the necessity of a solid education. We'd spend an hour each day in the Rotary library working on our communication skills. Lindsey tutored several kids, including Walter Greer, my cousin Bruce Harrell, and me. His teachings had a tremendous impact on our lives: Walter has a successful career at the Boeing Corporation and is a devoted family man; Bruce was an academic all-American football player at the University of Washington, and today he owns a successful law practice in Seattle.

Whenever he was around, Lindsey drilled me on different basketball fundamentals, like passing, dribbling, and shooting; and he'd also have me participate in his strenuous, customized conditioning program. One time he had me run more than ten miles all the way down to Seward Park, and when we got there, he had me jump into Lake Washington—shoes, clothes, and all—and run sprints in the water. Of course I did it . . . and then I had to run all the way back.

One of the things I remember most about Lindsey's guidance and direction is that each morning before we actually began practicing, he'd read us "The Scroll Marked III" from the book *The World's Greatest Salesman* by Og Mandino:

I will persist until I succeed.

I was not delivered unto this world in defeat, nor does failure course in my veins. I am not a sheep waiting to be prodded by my shepherd. I am a lion and I refuse to talk, to walk, to sleep with the sheep. I will hear not those who weep and complain, for their disease is contagious. Let them join the sheep. The slaughterhouse of failure is not my destiny. . . .

Nor will I allow yesterday's success to lull me into today's complacency, for this is the great foundation of failure. I will forget the happenings of the day that is gone, whether they were good or bad, and greet the new sun with confidence that this will be the best day of my life.

So long as there is breath in me, that long will I persist. For now I know one of the greatest principles of success: if I persist long enough, I will win.

I will persist.

I will win.

As Lindsey read these words each day, I became more and inspired to do whatever it took to be a champion. I was particularly impressed by what Og Mandino said about the value of persistence. I'd listen and think, *I'll stay in the gym all day if that's what it takes to be the very best I can be.* I couldn't wait for the real season to begin.

When basketball started up again my senior year, it looked as if everything was coming together. Again, we were touted as the team that would win the city championship. We were also rated number one in the state. This fueled speculation that we'd win it all. We still had JoJo Rodriguez, Larry Griffin, and Leon Johnson, as well as an incoming senior, Ronnie Mitchell—one of the best guards in the city. He lived up the street from Garfield, and we were thrilled when he transferred there.

But what was really different about this team was our new set of goals: We wanted to win the division, the holiday tournament, the city championship, the regional championship, and ultimately, the state championship.

Our head coach was Fernando Amorteguy; also on our coaching staff was Al Hairston, who'd played professionally with the Seattle SuperSonics. He made a tremendous difference in our offense, teaching us to effectively exploit our skills. Add to the package Ray Jones, who'd been coaching me on and off since the eighth grade, and we had a truly outstanding coaching staff who knew how to get along with each other and how to get the best out of us. One by one we looked at each individual goal. "We won't get ahead of ourselves," the coaches wisely instructed.

The season began, and we took off with a string of victories. I remember one game in particular against the Cleveland Eagles—they'd been billed as one of the best teams in the city because they had three "super sophomores" who'd played together since elementary school (and I had great respect for one of those underclassmen, Carl Ervin). The game was played in their gym, but we had focus. We put the press to their team, and they never had a chance. The score at the end of the first quarter had us in the lead, 25-0. They hadn't scored a point. By halftime, the score was something like 54-6. We blew them out of their own gym, and we made our statement on the court: We were the best team in the city.

By season's end, we were the city and division champs, and it was time to go to the playoffs. The holiday tournament was especially sweet for me because we were going to play a team with whom we had a score to settle. . . .

Back at the beginning of my senior year, a newspaper photographer wanted to take a picture of two "all-stars"—myself and a guy named Kim Stewart from Ballard High School. I recall being bothered that I had to go out to his high school for the photo shoot, and when I met Kim, he was a little cocky. Of course, I was a little cocky, too, so this led to some taunting.

"I'd just *love* to play Garfield High School," Stewart bragged as we were posing for our picture.

"No, you wouldn't," I responded under my breath. "You don't want to play us."

I went back to school and relayed the conversation to my teammates. We didn't forget that he made that comment, and, sure enough, it was Kim Stewart and the Ballard High School team that we were competing against in the holiday tournament.

"All-Star versus All-Star Team" was how the newspaper promoted the matchup. Kim's problem was that *he* was the all-star, whereas our entire team was made up of all-stars. In all fairness, I have to say that he played a great game—he may have been one of the best talents to ever come out of Washington State. But his effort alone wasn't enough. He got the points, but his team got spanked.

Then we went to the city championship . . . and who were we pitted against? Once again, it was Ballard and their superstar, Kim Stewart. By now, the Garfield Bulldogs were being referred to as the "Super Dogs." The headline in *The Seattle Times* read: "Super Dogs versus Kim Stewart and the Ballard Beavers." And, as in the holiday tournament, we ended up beating them.

Next we were headed toward the state tournament, where we'd face the Lincoln High School team from Tacoma. The *Seattle Post-Intelligencer* ran a story on our team as we approached the state championship. "The Super Dogs are probably the best team ever to play high school basketball in the state of Washington," it said. The same article quoted Lincoln's coach as saying, "We probably shouldn't even show up."

But *we* showed up. We knew that we were only two games away from the championship. "If we win this game, we're going to the state finals," we told each other. We came out confidently in the first quarter, but something wasn't clicking. Lincoln must have been scouting us from the first game of the season, because everything we tried to do, they shut down.

As the halftime buzzer sounded, we were behind. We ran off to the locker room in a daze. We hadn't lost a game the entire season—in fact, the closest we'd been to a loss was *winning* by eight points. And that had happened only once! We had to regroup. We couldn't come this far and fall short.

We came out for the second half committed to taking the lead, but at the end of the third quarter, we were still down. We could feel the mood of the spectators; it was as if they were collectively thinking, *Uh-oh, they're going to lose it again, just like they did last year.*

With only three minutes left in the game, we were still down by eight points. In a high school game with no shot clock, that meant trouble. (In college and professional basketball leagues, players have a limited amount of time to make a shot once their team gains possession of the ball. If they fail to do so, the defensive team is awarded control of the ball.) If Lincoln could freeze the ball for the remainder of the game, we'd be the losers.

Coach called a time-out. As I walked over to the bench, I saw something in my teammates I hadn't seen all season . . . defeat. It looked to me like they'd given up. "We can't win," was the message I heard, so something had to be done.

My coaches were all huddled over by the sideline, trying to come up with a strategy that would turn the game around. It didn't seem to be going well—they were bickering back and forth.

There I stood, thinking, *I practiced all year for this tournament.* And that's when I took over. I just looked at my coaches and teammates and yelled, "Give *me* the ball!"

Coach Amorteguy looked as shocked as everyone else, but he saw the determination in my face. "Okay, that's the play we're going to run. Let's go out and give Keith the ball!"

We came out of the time-out, and the offense ran through me. I turned around from 18 feet out, and *swish*—two points. Then we went into a one-three-one press, making me the first guy the Lincoln team had to get by. As soon as their man made his move, I stole the ball right out of his hand, made a reverse layup, and just like that, we were down by only four.

Lincoln brought the ball down, took a shot, and missed. Now we were back on offense, and once again, my teammates got the ball to me. I banked it off the glass from about 15 feet out. As Lincoln was bringing the ball up, I made another steal, shot the ball immediately, and it was good. The game was tied.

I was on fire. I knew we were going to win. Lincoln took a shot that circled the rim, and I outjumped everyone for the rebound. But as I was coming down, one of their players under-cut me and I fell, landing on my hip—hard.

The fans started running onto the court, and my team-mates encircled me. As I was lying on the floor, seemingly in a daze, everyone thought the worst. They huddled over me, ask-ing, "Keith, are you all right?" But I wasn't hurt, I was just savoring the moment. The game was truly in our control. We weren't going to lose now; I just knew it.

Curled up on the gym floor still clutching the game ball, I looked up at everyone, smiled, and winked. "Oh, I'm all right," I said. I couldn't feel any pain. I had two foul shots to make, and all I could think was, *Wow—we have this game won.* I didn't care what the guy was trying to do by undercutting me.

So I got up, brushed myself off, and went over to the foul line. I hit both shots, and we were up by two.

In the end, we won the game by eight points. I personally

had 28 points and double-digit rebounds. The fans exploded. I remember Clarence Acox, the band director at Garfield High, pulling me aside and saying, "Today you played like an all-American. Today you took over." That meant a lot.

Coach Bike, an assistant at Seattle University, was waiting for me when I left the locker room. "What a heck of a game you played—you were unbelievable! Best game I've ever seen a high school player play. You took the game into your own hands."

But the best compliment came from a man who was waiting to talk to me up in the stands—my dad. "Hey son, come up here!" he shouted excitedly. He extended his hand and said, "Boy, what a game. You played great!" I was so pleased to hear those words. There was no critique, just pure praise.

This time when I left the arena, I had no interest in walking home. I deserved to ride that bus.

The following night was one I'd dreamed about since I was 14 years old. It was the night I'd written about in all those yearbooks back in junior high. The Garfield High School basketball team was going to win the state championship.

Our opponent was Richland High. They'd played in the state final the year before but lost to Roosevelt High. Yes, James Edwards and his team had gone on to win the state championship after they defeated us. I felt that Richland had an advantage in having been to the finals already, so I decided to say a few words to my team in the locker room before we went out to play the game.

"Remember our goals," I said. "We wanted to win the division, the holiday tournament, the city championship, and the regionals, and we've accomplished all those goals. There's only one left: We need to win the state championship."

The guys all nodded in agreement.

"We had a tough fight last night, but we won," I continued.

"We're not going to have a tough fight tonight—we're gonna play our game. We're going to take this championship back to Garfield High School. On the count of three, let's go get it. One, two, three! *Let's go get it!*"

It was beautiful. Everyone was in the zone, playing in synch. I knew it was the last game I'd play for Garfield, so every time I touched the ball I wanted to do something special. Coach called a time-out early in the game, and for the first time, he said, "Relax now, Keith. We have a long game ahead of us."

I guess he was a little nervous because I was spinning, twirling, and doing every smooth move I could think of, and he wanted to play it safe. But we kept our focus and did what we needed to do.

We won. We were the Triple-A Washington State High School basketball champions.

When the horn sounded to end the game, I had the ball, and I threw it in the air as high as I could. My cousin Clayton (Peanut) and my good buddy Calvin Saunders ran over to me and literally jumped into my arms. It was like you see on television—we were all running around looking for someone to hug.

The next day when I got up and went outside to get the newspaper, there were three copies on the porch. The headline read: "Triple-A High School Basketball Champions Garfield High School Super Dogs."

Our win had an amazingly positive impact on the students and teachers at Garfield, but it also affected the surrounding community as well. To this day, when the state tournament is played, the Seattle media always review Garfield High School's successes. If they go back to the '70s, they always bring up the 1974 Super Dogs, pointing to us as one of the best teams in the school's history.

Those victories still give me goose bumps when I think

about them because I know they were meant to happen. I thank God for the experience, and I'm grateful, because it made such a mark on my life and the lives of so many others—we set a standard for excellence and inspired several championship teams that have since come from my school. It's a proud tradition that's still imprinted on my mind.

▲ ▲ ▲

LESSON 10:
Whatever It Takes (W.I.T.)
▲ ▲ ▲ ▲ ▲ ▲ ▲ ▲ ▲

From Og Mandino's *The World's Greatest Salesman:*

I will persist until I succeed.

The prizes in life are at the end of each journey, not at the beginning; and it is not given to me to know how many steps are necessary in order to reach my goal. Failure I may still encounter at the thousandth step, yet success hides behind the bend in the road. Never will I know how close it lies unless I turn the corner.

Always will I take another step.

If that is of no avail I will take another, and yet another. In truth, one step at a time is not too difficult.

I will persist until I succeed.

Whatever it takes: That's what I learned from Director Lindsey Stuart at the Rotary Boys' Club the summer before my senior year in high school. In order to be successful you have to have a "Whatever It Takes" (W.I.T.) attitude. Outstanding motivational speaker (and my good friend) Les Brown always said, "It doesn't matter whether life knocked you down as long as you landed on your back, because if you can look up, you can get up!"

I stand 6'6", and that's a long way to fall—but that's exactly what happened at the end of my junior year when we lost the state tournament. I took the defeat personally. But from that defeat, I developed a W.I.T. attitude. I started looking at our past season and analyzed the games to determine what had worked and what hadn't. I wanted to change what wasn't working and do what I needed in order to improve, whether it was doing push-ups, taking ballet lessons (yes, I took ballet lessons), or going to the gym to work on parts of my game that needed improvement. It took long hours of practice, committing myself to do something every day to help my team and improve my skills. I was going to persist until I succeeded.

I've carried that same attitude throughout my career. Success often requires doing whatever it takes. "Whatever it takes" may mean working long hours, weekends, and holidays; sacrificing that new car or wardrobe so that your business can be sustained; or admitting that you're not always right and that others may have the answer. "Whatever it takes" requires you to stay focused on your goals and committed to your success.

I truly believe that if you develop a W.I.T. attitude, you'll be a champion at whatever you decide to do. In my senior year, the headlines of *The Seattle Times* read: "Triple A High School Basketball Champions Garfield High School Super Dogs." What will *your* headlines say?

CHAPTER 11

. . . .

Sick, Tired, and
Nearly Defeated

*"Be glad for all God is planning
for you. Be patient in trouble,
and always be prayerful."*
— Romans 12:12

"It's your decision, Keith. It's up to you." I still remember my father's words the day I signed the paper that Bill O'Connor had brought over. Sitting there in the living room with my parents, I made my choice—I'd be attending Seattle University. Yet I had no idea that in a short amount of time, drastic changes would take me from the top floor of life to the basement.

Bill O'Connor was the head basketball coach at Seattle University, and he said all the right words. I hadn't really evaluated the university's basketball program; instead, I'd evaluated the coach and his staff. When Coach O'Conner told me that I'd "start" as a freshman, I couldn't resist—I guess my ego created a sort of tunnel vision.

That summer, I devoted a large amount of time to preparing myself for the college team. I was in good shape, so when official practice began, I was pleased with my performance. It was a good thing that I was physically prepared, because there were other challenges I'd face . . . on and off the court.

We had a freshman class filled with potential: The university had recruited Kevin Suther from Issaquah, Washington; Jerome Maultsby from Norwalk, Connecticut; Carl Washington from Stockton, California; and Doug Gribble from Mercer Island, Washington. Returning students included Reggie "Mean" Green, a sophomore who'd started as a freshman; along with Jerry "Horse" Lee, a junior college transfer.

Yet in spite of all that promise, it was clear from the start that the entire basketball program at Seattle University revolved around one player—Frank Oleynick. A bona fide college all-American (and our team captain), he was nicknamed "The Magic Man," and he *was* magic on the court. He was a junior when I joined the team, and rumor had it that he was leaving school early to turn pro.

I'd already played some pickup games with Frank during summer league, so I knew he was good. He shot the ball well, his passing abilities were excellent, and everyone looked up to him. I thought it would be a real treat to play with someone of Frank's caliber.

But Frank had his own ideas about our team. It quickly became apparent that *he* was the star, and he was going to continue being one by making sure that all the plays ran around him and through him. Now don't misunderstand, he really was a great player, but it was all about Frank. He wanted to be sure that each game showcased his talents for all the scouts who watched him and that he got his points. And the coaches catered to his whims.

Nevertheless, I was pumped up for the first game of my college career. It felt so good to be playing for a team that had actually recruited me to play. The excitement wore off, however, when I ended up only scoring eight points against the other team, UC Berkeley's Golden Bears. During one play, I got the rebound after a shot by one of my teammates. I should have put it right back up, but I passed it. Our team didn't make the basket, and we lost the game by only a couple of points.

That was to be the first of many losses that season. Out of more than 20 games, we won only 5 or 6. It was disappointing—not just for the team, but for me personally. I sprained my ankle several times that year, which certainly contributed to the frustration I was feeling. I could never seem to get on track.

Overall, my freshman year was a humbling one. I accomplished my goal of starting all season, but I didn't shoot the way I had in high school, and I passed up a lot of opportunities to score. I think the coaches wanted me to be more aggressive on offense, but I lacked the confidence. I felt that it didn't matter; Captain Frank took the shots, since most of the plays were designed for him.

Bill O'Connor was a great recruiter, but he coached in a different way from what I was used to. And it was an especially difficult season for him. The year before, he'd been named "Coach of the Year," but a couple of good players who'd brought real leadership to the team had graduated, and he never really recovered from that loss. So when things went well, Coach O'Conner was a wonderful person to be around. But if there was a challenge on the team, or we weren't winning, it was difficult for him to communicate effectively.

For the first time in my "career," I had to deal with a lot of negative motivation. There was always a focus on what *wasn't* working instead of what was working or how to make it work.

It was the first time I'd ever dealt with that type of coaching style, and it just didn't work for me. I had to make a real effort to maintain a positive attitude.

Looking back, I should have spent more time working on my jump shot and offensive moves. My coach couldn't play the game for me. The bottom line: We all hated losing. We just wanted to win.

▲ ▲ ▲

College life required a series of major adjustments. Of course, I managed to maintain a certain level of comfort by continuing to live at home. One of the reasons I chose to go to Seattle University was the scholarship they offered me—I even got a check for room and board. Since I didn't live in the dorms on campus, I was basically getting paid to live with my parents.

But the college schedule was tough. The basketball team's travel schedule was more intense than I thought it would be, especially since players had to keep up with their studies and class assignments on the road. The professors didn't cut us any slack just because we were on the basketball team—we still had to do the academic work. And with the exception of the days the team had to travel, I went to class every day—I never missed one.

I took my books with me when the team traveled. I still had to study even if we had a bad game, and we were having bad games just about every night. I had to deal with something I'd never dealt with before: the agony of defeat.

For most of my basketball career, I'd been the team captain. It used to be that when I walked into a classroom, people would start congratulating me on a good game. But that all changed. Most people didn't talk to us players at all because we were *losers,* but if they did, they'd say things like, "How come you're not winning? What's wrong with the team?" or "Frank got 36 points last night—why can't anybody else score?"

At the time, I though I'd lost my confidence. Yet I realize now I hadn't *lost* my confidence, I'd simply *misplaced* it. And I couldn't seem to find it on the basketball court.

The summer between my freshman and sophomore years, I dedicated myself to the gym in order to rebuild my confidence and improve my game. One of the assistant coaches, John Burnley, had a key to the gym at the Connelly Center (where we practiced during the season). He let me in, and it was just like back in high school at the Rotary Boys' Club. Coach Burnley and I would stay until midnight some nights, playing one-on-one, shooting jump shots, and talking a lot of trash.

This year will be different, I'd tell myself. So I worked hard that summer—really hard. Little did I realize that I was pushing myself so hard I was wearing my body down. I'd leave the gym all hot and sweaty and drive home in my Datsun 610. Being a college student, I didn't have a lot of money, let alone enough for a new set of wheels. I remember many a late night driving home in that old car with a broken heater and a crack in the window, cold air blowing right through my sweaty body. It was a scenario that would later come back to haunt me.

But at the time, my hard work seemed to be paying off. Frank Oleynick, as promised, left school early to play in the NBA with the Seattle SuperSonics, and the team elected three players to be captains: Reggie Green, Bucky O'Brien, and me. This was great news, especially since I got along so well with Reggie.

Reggie "Mean" Green's moniker was a result of the audible growl he emitted whenever he grabbed a rebound. He roared on the court, but off the court Reggie was one of the funniest and most likable people I've ever met. Known for his practical jokes, it wasn't uncommon to be engaged in a serious conversation when Reggie would quietly sneak up behind the person you were talking to and start making weird faces or mocking the person's gestures. The more you attempted to ignore his antics, the more outrageous he'd become. Eventually you'd crack up, and the person you were talking to would look perplexed, turn around, and see Reggie standing there straight-faced, as if he'd just walked up. It was all in good fun—he was always trying to get people to lighten up.

Reggie had a real knack for making people feel comfortable. No one was a stranger to him. We became good friends and roommates during my senior year. He was the product of a close and loving family, and his parents, John and Bernadyne Green, would invite the entire basketball team over to their house for fried chicken and peach cobbler whenever we played teams in the San Francisco Bay Area. (Nothing can replace the good times Reggie and I shared together—we're friends for life. Simply put, Reggie is a great person.)

Now we had cohesive team leadership. *Things are going to be different,* I thought. *The three of us will see to that. I'll just come out and play my very best—that's all I can do.* But that's when it happened . . . I got extremely sick.

I kept coming down with what seemed like the flu, but it would linger on, then worsen. Finally, the doctor figured it out. "Keith, you've got pneumonia," he said.

"What can I do to get better?" I asked.

"Rest," he replied. "That's all you can do. I'll prescribe some penicillin, but you've just got to go to bed."

"But I'll miss so much practice," I protested.

"I know, Keith. I'm sorry," was all the doctor could say.

A horrible pattern began to develop. I'd rest for a few weeks, return to practice again, get sick again, and have to sit out. Each time the doctor examined me, he'd extend my rest period.

The first game of the season was against our rivals, the University of Washington Huskies. They beat us twice my freshman year, and I'd played terribly both times. As a matter of fact, I'd set a personal record in one of our meetings—I played an entire game without scoring a point. *This year it's gonna be different,* I continued to repeat to myself.

During this game, I ran up and down the court a few times, but it was obvious that I was hurting. I was trying to guard a guy named Clarence Ramsey, an all-conference player and great shooter with very good head fakes. I remember thinking, *Don't fake anymore, Clarence, just shoot!* I was completely exhausted from guarding him.

Finally, Coach O'Conner had to take me out because I was so fatigued. I was really determined to play, but my body was too weak. I could barely bend down to tie my shoe without having to take a rest. We ended up losing the game by a couple of points.

Once again, I became very sick. This time the doctor said, "Keith, you have pleurisy. You need more rest." So I sat out another month.

By midseason, I'd played a few minutes of only one game. I still couldn't regain my strength, and the doctors were doing all sorts of tests on me, trying to discover what was really wrong.

A specialist was brought in to test me for sarcoidosis. According to the National Heart, Lung, and Blood Institute, sarcoidosis is a disease caused by inflammation. It can affect almost any part of the body, but it's usually found in the lungs. It makes small lumps to appear in the affected tissue, and these lumps can cause scarring. No one knows what instigates sarcoidosis, and in many cases, it just disappears as mysteriously as it appeared. There is no cure, and in chronic cases, severe scarring in the lungs and other vital organs can even be fatal.

The specialist found symptoms of the disease in my eyes.

AN ATTITUDE OF GRATITUDE

"Keith," he said, "I can't tell you that you have it, but I can't tell you that you *don't* have it. All I can say for certain is that you have symptoms similar to sarcoidosis."

When the coaches heard the doctor's diagnosis, they approached me with an idea. "You need some time to let your body heal," they told me. "We want to petition to redshirt you." (When college athletes are redshirted, it means that they must sit out a year, but that their eligibility will be extended.)

"Will I be granted an extension?" I asked skeptically.

"We don't know, but it's obvious that you're in no condition to play now. It's certainly worth a try."

So the school petitioned the National Collegiate Athletic Association (NCAA), and I was granted another year of eligibility. They made it clear that they would have denied the request had it been for pneumonia or pleurisy—they were granting the petition because of sarcoidosis.

▲ ▲ ▲

Losing all my strength was frustrating. So was experiencing life without basketball. Even though the NCAA gave me a fifth year to play, I'd promised my dad that I'd earn my degree in four years. I forced myself to keep up with my schedule even though I was sick. I can recall driving over to campus, finding a parking spot about four blocks away from the classroom, and being *drenched* in sweat by the time I got to class.

Certain lessons were becoming clear to me during this time. In the past, I'd been concerned about playing the game, about starting, and about points; now my attention shifted to waking up, walking, and living. I didn't even think about basketball—I didn't go to practice or hang out with my basketball buddies, and I didn't listen to any of our games on the radio.

• • • 110 • • •

There were no reporters to talk to, and no cheerleaders scream-ing my name.

Fortunately, since I'd stayed in Seattle, I had a built-in sup-port system. Family and friends helped me make the adjust-ment. There was Calvin Saunders, my friend since the age of 12, who'd drop by the house and take me out just to get my mind off my illness; Darrell Franklin, who lived across the street, and was like a younger brother to me; and Jeff Dowdle, who was always there to cheer me up. I was blessed to have car-ing friends to lean on during this time of tremendous change and disappointment. But for the most part, it was just me talk-ing to me . . . and of course, my mom.

One night I heard my mother crying. "Mom, what's wrong?" I asked, standing in the doorway of her bedroom.

"I feel so helpless—it pains me to see you sick. I know what basketball means to you. You've worked hard for this, and now everything seems so uncertain," she answered.

"It's okay, Mom," I said, trying my best to comfort her.

"I'm hurt and disappointed," she went on, "because *you* must be hurt and disappointed that you can't play."

I gave her a big hug. "Everything's gonna be all right," I assured her. "This is a challenge—we've been through chal-lenges before. We can beat this thing. I'm focusing on my strength and health. I'll be back, Mom, don't you worry."

But Grandma had a different take on things. She'd been a nurse, and my father had suffered from sarcoidosis when he was younger. "Your body is just worn down," she told me. "You stayed up all night shooting baskets, and you drove home all hot and sweaty in the freezing air. You didn't eat right. You came back from pneumonia too fast—it zapped your strength and you never gave your body time to heal. But you don't have sarcoidosis."

"I don't?"

"No. Just eat right and get your rest. God's gonna take care of everything."

I believed her. People started hearing that I had sarcoidosis, and, naturally, they'd ask me about it. "I don't have it," I'd tell them. "I just need time to rest."

They all just shook their heads. I guess they thought I was in denial. But guess what? Grandma was right. After about five months of rest, I began to feel better and regain my strength. My sophomore year came to an end, and despite my illness, I still managed to complete all of my course work.

I was so thankful because God had taken care of everything.

▲ ▲ ▲

LESSON 11:
Open Up Your Eyes
▲ ▲ ▲ ▲ ▲ ▲ ▲ ▲ ▲

When you're faced with setbacks or the prospect of defeat, how you view your circumstances influences your ability to reach your goals—and sometimes you just need to open up your eyes to help you get a new perspective. As the old saying goes: "When life hands you lemons, make lemonade." If you don't, you'll be left with nothing but a sour taste in your mouth.

Life was handing me basketfuls of lemons. I went to Seattle University to be a starter on a winning team—instead, I faced defeat. I was confronted with situations I hadn't dealt with before, including a coach who was so focused on one player that he failed to motivate the other members of the team, and an illness that left me unable to play ball.

But my personal struggles forced me to open my eyes and take a different look at what really mattered. And while my goals and dreams were still important, I realized that life, health, family, and friends were truly what it was all about.

So when life hands you a few lemons (and as I've said before, it *will*), look at your circumstances from a different viewpoint. It's sometimes a challenge to look beyond tragedy or failure and see blessings in their midst, but the ability to do so is ultimately the difference between winning and losing in the game of life.

CHAPTER 12
· · · · · · · · · · · · ·
Painting Alaska

*"Seek God's will in all you do, and
He will direct your paths."*
— Proverbs 3:6

"Let's go up to Alaska and work on the pipeline!" my
buddy Reggie Green suggested.

"Are you serious?" I asked.

"Yeah! Mr. Bergman, one of my old professors, is in
charge of a project up there. He said that if we can't get work
on the pipeline, he'll hook us up. It'll be a fun way to spend
the summer."

So the summer after my illness, I went exploring our 49th
state with Reggie. Mr. Bergman came through with some work
since we couldn't get hired on the Trans-Alaska Pipeline.

Reggie and I returned to Seattle midway through the summer and worked out in the gym, getting ready for the upcoming season. My strength was back, I was feeling good, and I
couldn't wait to play again.

I ended up having a very decent year, averaging 12 points

per game, and I was injury free the entire time. Once again, I was elected captain, and we added Clint Richardson to our team, who was chosen all-conference (and later all-American). I'm proud to say that we won more games than we did the previous year, but I knew we could be better still.

The next year was even more promising. We brought in two outstanding freshman, Carl Ervin and Jawann Oldham. We won our first couple of games, and things were looking up. But, as so often happens, injuries created extra challenges for our team, and to put it bluntly, we fell apart. To make matters worse, I wasn't playing up to my potential.

One particular game that stands out in my mind was an away game against the University of Portland—I remember it well because my family, including my grandmother, drove all the way down from Seattle to watch me play. I had a horrible game, and I didn't score a single point. I was so frustrated because I wanted my grandma to see me do well.

When the game was over, our defeated team went back to the visiting locker room, where Coach O'Connor had some choice words for us. There was a great deal of pressure on him to win games, and he was always pushing us to do better (and rightly so). But this time, he really chewed us out. And it got personal when he singled me out for not doing what I should have done. It was the first and only time I can remember being put down in front of my teammates, and it was terrible.

On the way home from the game, I started tossing the idea around that maybe I should give up basketball. For the first time in my life, I contemplated whether or not it was worth it for me to play for someone I couldn't do a great job for. I'd made major adjustments in trying to master O'Conner's coaching style, and I felt that I'd really tried my best.

I don't want to play anymore, I thought. *I don't want to play for a coach like that—somebody who demoralizes rather than motivates. He doesn't care about me, and he doesn't understand me either.*

I followed up that mental discussion by not going to practice the next day. Or the day after. I knew the newspapers were calling and so were my coaches, but I wouldn't answer my phone because I didn't want to talk to anyone.

Finally, assistant coach John Burnley got through to me. "Keith," he said over the phone, "we've got a road trip coming up this weekend. Just get your stuff and I'll see you on Thursday." Missing a couple of practices was one thing; missing a game was quite another.

I got on the bus, went to the game, and played. Coach O'Conner never said anything to me about missing practice, but Coach Burney had a few thoughts for me. "There's no quitter living in you," he said. "You won't walk away from a challenge, and you won't walk away from your commitment."

His words helped bring things back into focus for me. *Okay, Keith,* I told myself, *it's not right to walk away—that's just the easy way. The right way is to learn from all this, deal with it, and turn it around.* Coach Burnley reminded me that I'd made a commitment to the team—I'd given my word and I needed to honor it.

Looking back, I realize I was asking myself a question everyone asks at some moment in his or her life: *Do I have what it takes?* It was a turning point for me, and I had to reevaluate my priorities. I did manage to turn my attitude around, but I was still disappointed in the year we had.

None of that seemed to matter on the beautifully sunny afternoon in June 1978 when I graduated from Seattle University with a bachelor of arts degree in community service. The occasion was special for an obvious reason—I was thrilled to be graduating with my class. But on that day I also learned a lot about friendship from two very special people in my life, my former girlfriend Cheryl Burgess and my good buddy Raymond Austin.

Along with my family, they sat in the seats of the Seattle Center Arena (the same place my high school commencement ceremony had been held only four years prior) and cheered as I walked across the stage to receive my diploma.

After the ceremony, while my family and classmates congratulated me and we posed for photos, Raymond made his way through the crowd to give me a high five. He was genuinely happy about my accomplishment and celebrated it as if it were his own. I found his gesture particularly touching because he hadn't attended college.

Since the young lady I was dating at the time was nowhere in sight (later on I learned that she hadn't even attended the ceremony), I asked Raymond to join my dad; my stepmother, Gretchen; and me for dinner at Black Angus. That was a special meal. I'll always remember how proud Dad was—I'd kept the promise I made to him and myself by graduating in four years.

It was still early when Raymond and I said good-bye to my dad and Gretchen, so we decided to drive over to Seward Park. We cruised along Lake Washington in Raymond's classic Mercedes-Benz, talking, reflecting on the past four years, and dreaming about the future. It was a great way to end the day.

When I returned home, I noticed that someone had left a gift on the porch. It was from Cheryl, whom I hadn't seen at the graduation ceremony. Even though we weren't dating any longer, she wanted to let me know how happy she was for me. That's what I consider to be a sign of true friendship. Through their thoughtfulness, Cheryl and Raymond made my special day more memorable.

▲ ▲ ▲

So I had my degree, but there was still a question hanging over my head: Did I really want to return to Seattle U in order to play ball for my final year of eligibility?

There was some big news regarding the basketball program. Over the summer, Coach O'Connor announced he wasn't coming back. A new coach named Jack Schalow was hired, and our first meeting was very significant.

"Young man," he began, "I've had a chance to watch some game films, and I've seen how you play. I've heard people talk about you, and I'll tell you what: You've got talent. You've got good skills, and I want to *maximize* them. I don't think that's been done yet, do you?"

"Not really," I replied in total honesty.

"I can see you playing guard for me."

"Guard?" I said.

"Yes. I'd love for you to come back and play. I'd love to make you captain of the team. Will you think about it?"

I didn't need to think too much. I'd *always* wanted to play guard. I had visualized myself being a 6'6" guard from the time I was a little boy. Even though this meeting was my first with Jack, I believed him and trusted him. I made my decision right there on the spot. "Coach, I'd love to."

It was a great decision. The team had a new coach and a new attitude. Clint Richardson (who played eight years in the NBA and earned a championship ring) and I were named captains, and we won our first five games. I was shooting a really high percentage, my confidence was back, and as an added bonus, I was playing guard for the first time in my life.

I remember praying at the beginning of that final season: *Dear Lord, just bless me with a good year where I don't get hurt, the team can win some games, and I can leave Seattle University proud of the fact that I gave my all.* I'm grateful that He gave me exactly that.

I played guard for the first half of the season and benefited greatly from Coach Schalow and our assistant coach, Eddie Miles, a former Seattle U and NBA star.

Midway through the season, Ray Potlonga, a starter, left the team, so Coach needed to move me to forward. "This is a hard decision, Keith," he told me. "I know you've been playing well at guard, but the team needs you to play forward."

"I'll do whatever you think is best," I responded. So I moved to forward.

The team fell into a little slump, and we didn't finish as strongly as we'd hoped. But we won 16 games that year, and I had a 16-points-per-game average (the best of my college career), along with my personal best in shooting percentage.

In June of 1979, the NBA draft began. I'd spent most of my young adult life chasing the dream of becoming a professional basketball player, and family, friends, teammates, and others who'd followed my career had come to expect that I'd get selected in one of the ten rounds. It was common knowledge that each year the Seattle SuperSonics drafted a senior from either Seattle University or the University of Washington. Since I'd started all four years, I was a logical choice. I waited patiently by the phone through the early rounds, but it didn't ring. I waited and waited as the lower rounds were completed, but there was no call.

It was no ordinary year. The Seattle SuperSonics had just won the NBA Championship, and Coach Lenny Wilkens drafted only two players, forfeiting the team's other eight rounds because he knew no one else would be able to make it. It was the year that guys like Larry Bird and Magic Johnson entered the NBA, so needless to say, competition was tough.

Knowing that didn't make it any easier for me to accept my

disappointment. It was a difficult time in my life. I was devastated, angry, and bitter. I felt disconnected from life. My self-confidence and self-esteem took a dive.

▲ ▲ ▲

Question: What does a guy do when he's got his degree, finished his eligibility to play college basketball, hasn't been drafted to play in the NBA, and isn't very clear on what his next step should be?

Answer: He goes to Alaska to become a painter.

My aunt Sue was working in Anchorage. She offered to get me a job with her boyfriend, a painter who had a contract at Elmendorf Air Force Base. It sounded good to me—I wanted to get away from Seattle, where everyone seemed to know me *and* my disappointments. So I moved to Alaska, joined the painters' union, and attempted to clear my mind and regain my focus.

Painting was difficult work. I'd get up early every day, put on a pair of white coveralls that the union required us to wear, and go paint a building. Most days I got more paint on *me* than I did on the walls, so eventually they made me the "prep guy." My job was to make sure that everything was prepared for the guys who did the actual painting.

It really was a good time to clear my head, and I became certain of one thing almost immediately: I didn't want to be a painter the rest of my life.

I take my hat off to professional painters. It's a skill, and I didn't have it. It was about 74 degrees in Anchorage that summer, but it felt like it was over 100. Every day I felt hot and tired. I laughed when I realized that with the tan I was getting, by the time I returned to Seattle, people were going to think I'd been on some tropical island, not painting in Alaska.

To this day I'm grateful for Aunt Sue, her hospitality, and her encouragement. I ate dinner with her every night, and I remember how much we laughed. It was a great way to get my mind off basketball and just be thankful for life.

But wouldn't you know it—just about the time I was getting my mind off basketball, the phone rang.

"Keith Harrell?" a Dutch-accented voice asked.

"Yes," I replied.

"I'm the coach for a professional basketball team here in Rotterdam, Holland. You don't know me, but I know *all* about you. I've seen a few of your game films, and I'd like to offer you a position with our team."

I'd considered the option of playing overseas. My former college teammates Reggie, Bucky, and Kevin were all playing pro ball in Europe. I'd talked to Reggie at length about the challenges of living abroad, the league's salary structure, and the perks he received.

"Tell me more," I said to the coach.

"We're currently a division-two team in the European league," the coach went on to explain. "But if you play as well as I think you can, they'll move us up to division one."

"That's good." I stalled, wanting to collect as much data as possible.

"You know what happens here," he said. "You play well and you get noticed by the NBA. Next thing you know, you're playing professionally back in the States."

I'd heard of cases where that had happened, but they were the exception, not the rule. My buddies had told me enough about the European league that I knew to ask three important questions:

"Do I get a car?"

"No," the coach replied.

"Do I get to come home at all during the season?"

"No."

"Is it warm or cold over there during the winter?"

"Cold."

"Well, that's three strikes," I remember saying to the coach. "Will you let me think about it?"

"Yes, of course," he replied. "But, Keith, I'm afraid I can give you only 24 hours. If you aren't interested, I've got to recruit someone else instead."

"Okay, Coach," I said. "Call me back at this time tomorrow, and I'll give you my answer."

I'd pretty much made up my mind before I even hung up the phone. I really didn't have the desire to live in a foreign country, and I remember thinking, *The pay isn't very good, and I won't be close to any family or friends.* All that to chase a dream that was becoming more remote as time went by?

So when the coach called the next day, I politely told him, "Thanks, but no thanks." He said he understood, and I told him I was grateful that he'd worked so hard to track me down in Alaska.

That's when I made the decision to find a *new* game to play.

I'd worked hard all my life, and I had a persistent dedication and driving passion to win. I knew those traits would serve me well in any occupation, and especially in the business field. My future wasn't painting in Alaska, so I packed it up, kissed Aunt Sue good-bye, and moved back to Seattle.

Although my dad had always wanted me to major in business, I had never really been interested. Now, however, my attitude had changed. I shifted my focus from basketball to the business world. I began observing other successful people and started asking myself, *What has basketball brought to my life?* Three things kept coming to my mind as answers: I'd proved to myself that I was able to master the game; it had helped me gain self-respect and taught me the importance of respecting other people; and I'd learned about being part of a team and the camaraderie of working toward a common goal. I remember thinking, *Well, I can do all the same things in business.*

Once back in Seattle, I called my cousin Kenny Lombard. "Kenny, I'm ready to play another game."

"What are you talking about?" he asked.

"Basketball's been good to me, but I want to play the business game. I want to be successful. I think what basketball did for me then, business can do for me now. Do you know what I'm saying?"

"Yeah, I think I do."

"It's about success, and it's about working hard to accomplish a goal," I went on. "I think I'd like to work for the company you work for. Tell me who they are again?"

"IBM," he replied.

"I don't even know what IBM stands for, but I know you seem to be winning. You look prosperous, and I want to be, too. Do you think I have what it takes?"

My cousin was quiet for a minute, then he responded, "Keith, I believe you've got what it takes, but it's going to take even more effort than you put in at the gym to become a great business player. It's an extremely competitive marketplace."

Kenny kept talking, and I loved what I was hearing, because in my mind he was creating a parallel between business and sports: If you work hard at it, you'll succeed . . . as long as you don't allow fear or doubt to get in the way.

When I didn't get drafted into the NBA, I got scared. The reasons that I didn't go for a walk-on tryout for any of the teams or play in Europe were *fear* and *doubt*. I thought, *What if I still don't make it? How will it look?* So there I was, feeling like a failure.

But that wasn't the complete picture.

Faced with a new set of opportunities, I decided that I wouldn't let fear or doubt take control of me again. As I talked to Kenny about how to approach IBM, I knew there was no room for either.

That summer taught me much about life beyond basketball. I was through painting Alaska—I was ready to make *my life* a masterpiece.

▲ ▲ ▲

LESSON 12:
Setbacks into Setups
▲ ▲ ▲ ▲ ▲ ▲ ▲ ▲ ▲

For as long as I could remember, all I wanted to do was play professional basketball. In just one day—the day of the NBA draft in my last year of college basketball eligibility—that dream came to an end. Not just because I didn't get drafted, but also because I let the fear of failure keep me from setting up a new game plan.

I had the opportunity to try out as a walk-on for a number of NBA teams. I could have played ball in Europe for a few years and then tried again in the States. I realize now that it was my fear that caused me to walk away from basketball and go paint Alaska. By focusing on the innumerable "what-if-I-don't-make-it" scenarios, I didn't give myself a chance to succeed. I never took that leap of faith. I focused on what others might think or say and let thoughts of imagined rejection, potential embarrassment, and possible ridicule keep me from pursuing the thing I most wanted. What I should have done was let that setback set up a new game plan, and, ultimately, I did. But instead of the NBA, I chose IBM.

Whenever we listen to what critics or gossips say, we willingly give away our power of positive possibility. We're not born with a spirit of fear, but a spirit of power and love. So the next time you encounter a setback, use the power of your sound mind to turn it into a setup. Set a new goal, formulate a plan to achieve that goal, and take a risk. Don't let life's inevitable obstacles keep you from going after what you truly desire.

CHAPTER 13

· · · · · · · · · · · · · ·

International Business Machines (IBM)

"Look straight ahead, and fix your
eyes on what lies before you.
Mark out a straight path for your feet;
then stick to the path and stay safe."
— Proverbs 4:25–26

As fate would have it, IBM wasn't hiring at the time that Kenny and I had our first conversation, but he said, "Just because they're not hiring *now* doesn't mean we can't start the preparation."

"All right, I'm ready," I responded with enthusiasm. "Let's go for it!"

My success had always been a result of people coaching me, and I understood the value of mentors. Kenny was just a couple years older than I, but he was way ahead of me on the business scene. While I was painting in Alaska, he was moving up the corporate ladder. He'd come to IBM as a sales representative and had already been promoted to a position in marketing.

I was thrilled that he was willing to sign on as my mentor to help me get hired there. Just as I'd spent many hours in the gym warming up for a big game, I was ready to spend just as many hours in a study setting, preparing for my job interview.

"I'll give you every Saturday morning," Kenny graciously volunteered. "We'll practice interview skills, and you'll learn the company jargon and brush up on basic business issues. But listen to me, Keith: Since you're taking up my time, I'm going to hold you accountable for the work I want you to do before each of our meetings."

"Okay," I agreed, eager to do whatever was necessary to succeed in my new endeavor.

"I'm going to give you information to study, books to read, and problems to work on," he continued.

"I'll do it," I said.

"And one more thing," he added. "When we meet, I expect you to show up on time."

"I will."

"If you don't meet these criteria, I'll get in your face. Do you understand?"

I nodded.

Preparation for the first Saturday-morning meeting began days ahead of time when I received a phone call from Kenny. "I just wanted to remind you that you have an appointment with me this Saturday," he said.

"I know," I replied. "I'm looking forward to it."

"The appointment is at 8 A.M.," Kenny continued, "and here's what I want you to know. We're going to imagine that this is a *real interview* at IBM. I want you to pretend that you don't know me. So bring your résumé; park in front of my house; knock on the door; introduce yourself, and say that you have an 8 A.M. interview with Ken Lombard, the sales manager. Then we'll begin the interview."

"Great," I said, getting more excited as he spoke.

I tried my best to get ready for the "interview" all week. On Friday night, a couple of buddies called to see if I wanted to play basketball the next morning. "I won't be playing any Saturday-morning basketball for a while," I informed them.

"Why?" they asked.

"I'm practicing to get a job at IBM."

They snickered and said, "Tell us, Keith, how long do you have to 'practice' before they'll give you a job?"

Imagine their response when I admitted, "Well, they're not even hiring right now."

The laughter on the other end of the line was uproarious. "That's a good one."

"Yeah, well, listen up," I asserted. "I'm getting ready so that when they *do* begin hiring, I'll get the job."

▲ ▲ ▲

At a few minutes before eight on Saturday morning, I pulled my car up to Kenny's house. I walked to the front door, knocked, and was greeted very formally by my cousin.

"Yes?" he said, acting as if he didn't know me.

"My name is Keith Harrell," I began. "I have an eight-o'clock appointment with Ken Lombard."

"Please, come in and sit down," Kenny said as he led me into his office.

I followed him in, sat down, and was sure everything was off to a good start, when suddenly Kenny stopped pretending and looked straight into my eyes.

"THE INTERVIEW IS OVER!" he announced.

"Why?" I asked in disbelief.

"Look at the way you're dressed," he answered, pointing at my clothes.

I looked down at my outfit and thought, *I look pretty cool.* I was wearing blue suede shoes, a blue silk shirt with an open collar, and a gold chain around my neck. I was confused. "What's wrong with the way I'm dressed?"

"You look as if you're planning on steppin' out," Kenny said. "As if you're going to the disco, not IBM."

"So, what should I wear?"

"That's your assignment for next week." He smiled. "Two things: First, go out and buy a copy of the book called *Dress for Success,* by John T. Molloy, and read it. Second, on Monday morning I want you to go downtown and stand in front of the IBM building. See what the employees are wearing. *That's* how I want you to present yourself. So when you come back next Saturday, dress appropriately, and we'll continue. If you're not dressed right, I'll send you home again."

I couldn't believe it. "That's it for today?"

"Yes," Kenny replied. "It's over. Do you know why?"

"Why?"

"Because you *flunked.*" With that, he got up and showed me to the door.

Naturally, I went right out and bought *Dress for Success* and devoured it. Then I made sure that I was downtown early Monday morning as the IBM executives headed into their offices. And when I met with Kenny the next weekend, I didn't get sent home.

The Saturday sessions lasted for several months. Kenny did a wonderful job of coaching me, leaving no stone unturned. For example, he helped me a great deal with my diction—teaching me to talk like a business person and to lose the slang that was second nature when I spoke with family and friends. When I hung out with my friends, everything was "Yeah, man," or "Ya know."

"There's a difference between how you talk to an IBM customer and how you talk to your buddies when you're playing basketball," he told me.

I learned new business vocabulary and appropriate etiquette, as well as posture, presentation, and poise. It was as if I was working toward my MBA every Saturday morning. Plus, I learned more and more about the inner workings of IBM. I knew how sales were going in the Seattle office compared to other offices in the region, I could name the local managers and cite their successes during the prior year, and I gained a solid understanding of the structure of the company.

During this time in IBM's history, the company's workforce was divided into three different divisions: The Data Processing Division sold mainframe computers; the General Systems Division sold midrange computers; and the Office Products Division (always referred to as OPD by IBM employees) sold copiers, typewriters, word-processing equipment, and other office-related products. Inside IBM, this last division was considered the "lowest" of the three. I became very familiar with OPD because I was researching it on a weekly basis.

But besides turning me into a walking IBM encyclopedia, Kenny also helped me take an objective look at my strengths and weaknesses. He showed me how to counter any of my weaknesses by focusing on a strength. "I notice from looking over your résumé," he said, as if he were a manager interviewing me, "that you don't have a business degree. I also see that you haven't taken any computer or business courses."

I was ready with an answer. "Sir, my father teaches business classes at the college level, so I assure you, I know the importance of a balance sheet and an income statement, as well as assets and liabilities."

Kenny hesitated, "Yes, but . . . ,"

"Sir, if I may continue," I pressed on, "notice what I *do* have. I have leadership qualities that will lend themselves well to this position. I played varsity basketball at Seattle University for four years. And for three of those years I was the team captain."

"That's good," Kenny answered.

"I know the importance of learning about the competition. For example, I know that our competitors are Xerox, Wang, Lanier, and Kodak, to name a few. I know how important it is to learn about their offense and their defense so we can be victorious over them."

Kenny smiled. "Tell me more."

"The experience of being a team captain also taught me how to take charge. And I know that as a salesman, it's important for me to take charge of my customers and my territory and to make my quota. I want to do all I can to move the business forward."

Kenny was pleased with my response. "You've done a great job answering my questions. You've applied your strengths as a way of offsetting your weaknesses. I think it's time to set up a mock interview with somebody from IBM."

"That's great!" I exclaimed.

"A good friend of mine is the assistant to the regional manager here in Seattle. I want you to call him and schedule an appointment. Take your résumé with you, and as always, pretend that this is the real thing. Are you ready for this next step?"

"I believe I am," I answered.

The day of the "interview" arrived, and I went to visit Kenny's friend. I was nervous, but I knew I wanted this opportunity more than anything, so I just stayed focused and followed my game plan.

The interviewer asked me many of the questions that Kenny and I had gone over for weeks, and it felt good to know the appropriate responses. But I also remember him asking me a question that I hadn't anticipated: "Keith, how will you stay motivated in a job like this one?"

I answered this one without any help from my cousin. "Well, it's all about *setting goals*. I'll set goals to reach my sales quota, and I'll make it my mission to get promoted to marketing manager. I'll draft a variety of objectives that are both achievable and challenging enough to push me to maximize myself in this company, and reaching them will keep me motivated."

It was a natural response; after all, setting goals had served me well in sports and in earning my degree. The assistant to the regional manager was impressed, and the entire interview was a very positive experience. When it was over, he complimented me on how prepared I was. He offered two or three pieces of advice that would strengthen my interviewing techniques, and then agreed to meet with me again in about a month for another trial run.

I became obsessed: I was going to be hired by IBM, and nothing was going to get in my way. I spent the next couple weeks in constant study; as a result, the follow-up mock interview with the assistant to the regional manager went even better. In fact, it went so well that he made the following suggestion: "Keith, I think you're ready. So I'd like to set you up for a courtesy interview."

"Really?"

"Yes, but I emphasize *courtesy* because IBM is still not hiring. But we're always looking for potential talent somewhere down the line. Are you interested?"

"Absolutely—you tell me when and where and I'll be there."

An appointment was set, and I was on fire. Anybody who'd sit still long enough would get to hear my presentation for the interview. My mom heard it so many times she could quote it back to me. I made my pitch to my sister and to all my friends. I lived, ate, and slept that IBM interview.

I also stepped everything up a couple of notches with Kenny. We went from Saturday-only sessions to Saturdays plus two or three nights a week, and I went to the local library and studied in addition to that. I was as prepared as I could be. My meeting would be with Mr. Coby Sillers, an IBM manager in the sales division known for his thorough and intense style. He was tough, but I was ready.

"You didn't take any business courses in college, Keith," he began. "What makes you feel that you're qualified to come to work for IBM? What makes you equipped for a business like ours?"

I smiled, took a deep breath, and began. "Mr. Sillers, I spent four years in college, and I graduated on time. My major, community service, taught me how to deal with all kinds of people and how to build and manage relationships. These skills are especially important in today's market, where a successful businessperson has to cultivate partnerships, work as a member of a team, and know what it takes to win. I was a starter on my basketball team all four years in college, which proves that I'm a hard worker. I was the team captain for three of those years, which further demonstrates my leadership abilities and shows that I know about preparation and competition, and I have the right attitude. My dad's been teaching business for more than 20 years now at Seattle Community College, so I know the basics. I'm confident that I have what I need to do this job; and what I don't know, I can learn. I assure you, I can handle anything IBM asks me to do."

It appeared that the interview was going well. I was satisfied with my response, and I was delighted that I'd spent so much time in preparation for this session. Eventually, Coby Sillers got around to one of the questions that IBM considers crucial in all job interviews:

"Keith, how would you sell me this pencil?" He pointed to one lying on his desk.

"Mr. Sillers, before I sell you anything, let me take the time to understand exactly what your needs are. I want to sell you what you need, not what I *think* you need. My purpose in being here is to form a relationship—a partnership. So let me ask *you* some questions so I can better understand your needs."

Mr. Sillers liked my answer. We had another few meetings together, and then the process was considered complete. I had a good feeling. I'd prayed and I'd prepared—the rest of it was out of my hands.

I set my sights high, but the rest of my family had their doubts during the training process. My sister thought I was crazy; and to my amazement, my mom, who'd always supported me in everything, thought this was a far-fetched plan. She let me know in little ways, such as bringing home job applications for employers such as Boeing and the city of Seattle. Both offered great opportunities, but my focus was on IBM.

I honestly believed that IBM was the *only* company who could meet my needs. In my opinion, they were the best company in the world because they truly respected the individual and were all about performance, excellence, and striving to be the best with the customer. IBM so completely coincided with my sports philosophy that I was convinced it was Big Blue or nothing.

You can imagine how happy I was the day the phone rang. "Hello?" I answered.

"Is this Mr. Keith Harrell?"

"Yes, it is."

"Well, congratulations, Mr. Harrell. Your first day of work at IBM is October 17th."

▲ ▲ ▲

I'm so grateful to my cousin Kenny for all his help. In many respects, the two of us were peers, so I had to humble myself to even ask for his assistance in the beginning, but you never know who God will use in your life to make a difference. I realize that so much of my success was a direct result of all the time and energy Kenny and I put into preparing for my IBM interviews. It really *is* all about relationships when you stop to think about it.

▲ ▲ ▲

LESSON 13:
Input Equals Output
▲ ▲ ▲ ▲ ▲ ▲ ▲ ▲ ▲

Have you ever gone to a bank and attempted to make a withdrawal from an account in which you'd never made a deposit? Or have you ever tried to bake a cake without adding the proper ingredients? Of course not! It's common wisdom that you can only get *out* of something what you put *into* it. The same holds true for our goals in life.

When I was a boy, I believed that one day I'd overcome my stuttering. It was my goal. But in order to reach that goal, I had to go to speech therapy for six years and practice after school and during vacations. It required a lot of effort, energy, and practice to obtain my goal—in other words, input.

In junior high, I decided that I wanted to be an all-American basketball player and win the state championship in my senior year of high school. In order to do this, I had to put in long hours of practice, be coachable, and model other athletic stars.

Likewise, I did everything in my power to attain my goal of working at IBM. I attended the "Ken Lombard boot camp," studied the company, and developed the business lingo. I researched the industry and learned as much as I could about what went on day-to-day at IBM's Seattle office. I gathered information about the competition, tailored my résumé, and practiced my interview skills. I acted as if I were already an employee . . . and eventually I became one.

Everything in life that's worth having is worth working for. Remember the saying from Lesson 5: *There are no free lunches.* In order to obtain your goals—your desires in life—you must be willing to do whatever it takes to become successful. It may mean going back to college to get that degree you've been putting off, or taking special training courses to obtain a certificate. It may mean long hours at the office, or it may mean sacrificing some enterprise in order to have a peaceful and harmonious home.

Simply put, you get out of life only what you put into it: Input equals output.

CHAPTER 14

. . . .

Early Days at Big Blue

*"Commit your works to
the Lord, and then
your plans will succeed."*
— Proverbs 16:3

Going through training at IBM was like completing four years of college in a couple of semesters.

They called it "Internal Training," and to say it was thorough would be an understatement.

I was hired to work in the Office Products Division, or OPD. Training began with a 17-week course that covered IBM's history, products, and sales techniques. Some days we sat through lectures, and other days we role-played, but *every* day we took tests. Our performance was constantly assessed by different people in the company.

To add to the stress, the company policy was that if a new hire didn't pass the tests at Internal Training, they could be terminated. IBM was famous for its high standards, and the Seattle branch was known for producing some of the best salespeople in the country—intensity went with the territory.

After I completed my local training, I was shipped off to Dallas, Texas, along with new employees from all over the country. Here, we were to take the first of two additional classes, which had to be completed within our first year of employment, and only after passing them would we be considered "qualified" as sales reps.

Our instruction in these classes covered every last detail of how an IBM salesperson should promote the company's wares. We had to be able to demonstrate the entire product line, and we were drilled on selling features, functions, and benefits—we were even instructed on how to sit in our chairs and respond when spoken to. And of course, we were tested, critiqued, and graded.

An advisor was assigned to each of us, and it was that advisor's job to monitor our work, give us feedback, and report our progress to our training managers. Larry Childs, assigned to mentor me through basic training, was the best. He helped me until my salesmanship and presentation skills were right on the money, and my knowledge of written accounting techniques and product testing was just as it should be.

I felt a lot of extra pressure in Dallas because the last four people who'd gone through training from the Seattle branch had won the Marketing Excellence Award for being the "best of the best" in a class of about 40 students. So it was with a great sense of accomplishment and relief that I, too, won the award during my second week of training.

I remember how thrilled I was to call back to Seattle and tell Coby Sillers (the manager who'd hired me and was now overseeing my training) the good news. "Coby, I won the Marketing Excellence Award!"

"Congratulations, Keith, that's great!"

"I'll be back in Seattle soon, ready to go to work," I promised.

"Study hard, and we'll be waiting for you," Coby replied.

The day I finished Internal Training was an important milestone. I'd completed all the courses, passed all of the tests, and now I was finally ready to begin my career. This was my first real job out of college, and I was holding my own with the best of them. I was psyched.

At the time, I thought IBM was the perfect place for me. People who didn't know what was going on in my life would come up to me and say, "Aren't you playing basketball?" It had been a hard question for me to answer until the day I could happily announce, "No, I'm not playing ball, but I'm playing for IBM." And then I'd hand them my business card. I was extremely proud of being associated with such a successful corporation.

One day I was out at the gym shooting hoops, and an old friend of mine (who was a little out of touch) asked, "So, Keith, who are you playing for now?"

"IBM," I responded.

"Are they any good?"

"The best in the league! They win the championship every year."

"Wow! How many points are you averaging?

"A lot."

"Yeah?"

"That's right. I'm the MVP."

He was really impressed . . . although I later found out that he thought I was talking about some basketball team in Europe!

▲ ▲ ▲

Denny Holm was supposed to be my marketing manager when I returned from Dallas to Seattle, but for some reason plans were changed and I was to report to Coby Sillers. That was just fine with me, since he'd been my training manager and I felt as if we knew each other.

Coby gave me a territory and a quota and put me on an assignment. Being a rookie, I didn't feel very close to anyone in the company, except for two people who'd been trainees with me—Ralph Bianco and Kim Jorgensen. Ralph was my closest buddy at IBM, but he was 30 miles away in Everett, Washington, so he reported to a different manager. My cousin Kenny had left his position to begin a new career in commercial real estate, so he wasn't there anymore either. I later discovered that it was a real mistake to be a part of this huge company without seeking out any kind of mentor or coach.

My first year included a lot of "winging it," and I had to learn a lot of lessons the hard way. I'll never forget the first time Coby arranged for us to go out on sales calls together. It was embarrassing, because even though I did *exactly* what I'd been taught during training, this was the real world, and prospective customers didn't always respond in the way that trainees did in class. If they said they didn't have the money in their budget, they meant it. It was humbling for me to learn this in front of my boss, but I considered it all a part of the learning experience.

Six months later, Coby informed me that he'd join me on another call. I was a lot more confident, because by that time I felt that I was doing pretty well in my territory. But there was still a lot to learn. Looking back, I realize that I could have done a better job of showcasing my abilities. I could have prearranged certain calls that would have featured me in front of my best customers, and I should have had Coby with me on a guaranteed sale or at least a pickup of a signed order.

But I didn't do any of those things. Instead, Coby saw a typical day, which actually ended up being worse than usual. He went with me while I demonstrated one of our Model 75 electronic typewriters with 750 characters of memory. It was a new model that I hadn't worked with much yet, and my nervousness showed. At the next stop, the customer opened up the appointment with a complaint. Coby saw that, too. Later, I was to present a copier lease-to-purchase proposal to a customer, which was fine, but I wasn't the one who'd written up the sales proposal, which was *not* fine. It had been written by my copier specialist, Les Houle, who'd instructed me to deliver it to the customer. Coby asked me some challenging questions in the customer's parking lot that I couldn't fully answer. "Keith, why don't we go back to the office and create a proposal that you're totally comfortable with," he advised. We both decided that it wasn't the best time to make that sales call.

While it was embarrassing, it was actually a good experience for me, because Coby walked me through writing a proposal to convert copiers from lease to purchase. I took that proposal and used it to sell almost every one of the leased IBM Copier Model II's in my territory.

However, I couldn't help feeling that Coby had lost confidence in me. Then, when fellow rookie Kim Jorgensen and I began working long hours in the office together, I think Coby mistakenly concluded that the two of us were dating, which definitely put me in a bad light with him. Coby was somewhat paternalistic toward Kim, and while Kim deserved all the recognition she got, I felt slighted.

Kim also understood more about office politics than I did. After the day of her sales calls with Coby, I asked her, "How did it go?"

"Great!" she replied to my amazement.

"It did?"

"Couldn't have gone better."

"What did you do?" I inquired.

"Well, I typed up an agenda in advance detailing everything we'd do today. Coby was really impressed with that."

"He was?" I asked, suddenly realizing there were a number of things I still had to learn about this business.

"Yeah, he told me so during lunch."

"Lunch?" I was astonished. "You guys had lunch together?"

"Sure. It's right here on the agenda," she replied, pointing to an item in the middle of the page. "You didn't take Coby to lunch when he went out with you?" she asked.

"I didn't even think to do it," I admitted.

I was learning every day.

▲ ▲ ▲

The end of my first year came to a close, and everyone in the company was talking about the same thing . . . making quota.

IBM ranked their sales force based on performance, and they used the rankings to determine pay. At each year's end, sales reps were reviewed and given a number between one and five: A three was rewarded to a rep who made quota; someone who barely met quota got a four; and falling short resulted in a five (and the likelihood of not being around for next year's appraisal). A rep who exceeded quota was awarded a two, and a score of one was reserved for those who far exceeded quota—which was akin to walking on water. I was told that very few people ever received a one on their appraisal. When I heard that, I made it my aim to earn a one.

But as I looked over my totals for the year, I saw that I still hadn't reached my minimum. I wasn't far off, so I went to see Coby while there was still time to make a difference. The first thing he said was, "Let me see your control book."

I thought back to the beginning of the year when he'd first

asked me to put this book together. "What's a control book?" I'd asked.

He'd replied, "Keith, I want you to keep a record of every sales call you make, every demonstration you give, the products you have, and the status of those products."

Even though it was a lot of work, I put the book together, just as he'd requested, and I kept it up faithfully all year. And so, by looking at my book that day, Coby knew my precise situation.

"As you can see by my numbers, I'm a little short of making quota," I admitted. "But I'm still pluggin' away. I'm going to make it."

"I'll tell you what," Coby said, leafing through the book. "The truth is, the whole branch is doing poorly, so we've been given a quota reduction. I'm going to give you some of that reduction, and I think, using the new numbers, you should make it with no problem."

I went out there and sold like crazy for the last few days of the year. Kim and Ralph had already achieved their quotas, so they pitched in and followed up on some of my sales leads.

One of the biggest perks of making quota was membership in the 100% Club, which brought with it a trip to Miami for a few days of recognition, fun, and entertainment. All the sales reps looked forward to these trips, and Kim and Ralph were already guaranteed a spot. I wanted to be there as well.

By year's end, when the numbers were tallied, *I'd made it*. I celebrated by taking Kenny and his friend Mike Smith, who'd put me through my initial mock interview, out to a big dinner. It felt great to have come so far.

Not too long after the year's end came annual final evaluations, which determined numerical rankings as well as paychecks. I walked into Coby's office with a feeling of confidence and accomplishment.

"Keith, I think you should be really proud of yourself," he began.

"Thanks, Coby," I answered. "I'm pleased that I made my numbers."

"Yes, you did a good job. And because you did, I'm going to reward you with a four."

"A four?"

"Yes, a four. Since we had to lower your quota, I feel that you deserve the ranking that's best represented by a four. You barely made your quota, but you did make it and that should make you proud."

He was such a good salesman that I bought it. I left his office without challenging the ranking.

Later that day, I had a talk with another sales rep, Paul Stromire. "Did you get your ranking?" he asked.

"Yes, I did," I replied.

"What did you get?"

"I got a four."

"A four?" he asked. "Why only a four?"

"Well," I explained, "when Coby took a look at my control book—"

"Whoa, whoa!" he interrupted. "What's a control book?"

"It's the book where I record all my sales calls, demonstrations, products, and product status," I answered, matter-of-factly.

"Are you kidding me?" Paul asked.

"No. Why?"

"I've never had to keep anything like that. Let me take a look at it."

I showed him my control book, and he went through it page by page. "Keith, this is the most organized thing I've ever seen!" he exclaimed.

"Thanks," I said.

"You don't deserve a four. You deserve at least a three."

"You think so?"

"You didn't *barely* meet your goal—you *exceeded* it. If I were you, I'd go back in there and tell Coby Sillers what you think."

So I did. I went back into Coby's office, sat down, crossed my legs, and leaned over his desk. "Coby, I've been thinking about it, and I believe that I deserve a three."

He crossed his legs right back at me, leaned in, and said, "I want you to know that I have a lot of respect for your coming in here asking for a three. Actually, I have more respect for you now than I did before you asked."

"Thank you," I replied.

"But let me tell you why I'm not going to give you a three—I'm going to stick with my original ranking of four." Being the consummate salesman that he was, he sold it to me again. And that was the end of it.

When I found out that Ralph had gotten a three from his manager and that my co-worker Kim had received a two, I was really discouraged. We'd done the same numbers, and we'd all won the Marketing Excellence Award during training. I had enough insight to know that something was going on, and I began to wonder if it was personal. IBM had an open-door policy, which meant that an employee could go to upper management to question a decision, but I chose not to pursue that avenue because whether I won or lost, I thought it would be a bad message to send to my manager and the rest of the team. I'd also heard rumors that going up the line could leave a "scar" on my record that might affect my future with the company. So I just kept my mouth shut.

Years later, I still know that I deserved a three, but at the time, I didn't know what else I could do.

▲ ▲ ▲

In my second year at IBM, I was given a new manager. I didn't have that great a year, so I didn't make the 100% Club . . . but my manager still gave me a three. Go figure.

Yet the damage had been done by the four I got in the previous year. I'd have to wait longer for a raise and a promotion— I already felt as if I were behind the eight ball.

During my third year at Big Blue, two of the three sales divisions, OPD and the General Systems Division, were consolidated. It all happened suddenly, and before we knew it, we were being trained in the other division's products and services. Overnight I was learning about IBM's midrange computers and software applications, while the General Systems people were learning about electronic typewriters, copiers, and word-processing equipment. The merger of the two divisions created an overlap—two sales people, two different sets of skills, one sales territory. The number-one General Systems rep, John Lugwick, and I shared the same territory. John was the guy who sold the most midrange computers in the *entire country,* but rather than splitting our territory, management simply allowed John to continue selling all the computers, while I was stuck selling typewriters and copiers.

One day, a helpful manager took me aside. "Keith," he warned, "the handwriting is on the wall. If they won't give you any computer accounts, then you're not going to be able to make your numbers in the long run."

That's when I began looking at other options within the company. They'd recently opened a retail outlet, called the IBM Product Center Store, which sold copiers, typewriters, word processors, and the new personal computers. I considered my situation and thought, *Well, if they won't let me sell computers in my territory, then maybe I should sell them over at the Product Center Store.*

I knew some people at the store, including the manager, Jody Hughes, who was a great guy. My marketing manager helped me transfer, and I started working there soon after.

I just loved it. It was an exciting time for IBM. The personal computer was launched with a major ad campaign, featuring a guy who looked like Charlie Chaplin. We were hugely successful.

Now I was in retail sales. I was once again selling typewriters and copiers, but I was also learning how to sell personal computers. I was really enjoying myself, but we still had quotas to meet.

Achieving those goals was difficult because most of the sales were the luck of the draw. People walked into our store off the street, and the first available sales person would help them. There was no way to know whether a person was an interested buyer or someone who was "just looking," so sales were unpredictable.

Then there were the phone leads. I thought they'd be evenly distributed to the sales force, but it didn't take too long for me to realize that these leads were passed on by the administrators of the Product Center, and the administrators had their "favorite" salespeople. It was the same story with mail leads.

I didn't like the politics that I was seeing, but I knew that I'd be worse off as a sales rep. So I stayed on at the Product Center for the next three and a half years.

LESSON 14:
Promote Your Personal Résumé
▲ ▲ ▲ ▲ ▲ ▲ ▲ ▲ ▲

The camera is on you. You have one minute to do a "sound bite," a 60-second commercial to advertise your most valuable asset—yourself. Before anyone else will recognize your value, you must be able to see it. Be your own public relations firm promoting your personal résumé. Remember: Attitude is everything, and how you view yourself is how others will view you.

In my early days at Big Blue, I learned that customers often cared less about the brand name or quality of a product than they did about the person selling it. My failure came because I failed to promote *Keith*.

Our failures are opportunities to learn. Having an entrepreneurial spirit is about being able to assess your skills and then use them so that others can understand the benefits you bring to the table.

So, first you must know the product—*you*. You must be able to succinctly describe what I refer to as your features (skills), functions (what you do), and benefits (impact to the consumer). At a time when the economy is under attack, layoffs and unemployment rates are high, and playing the stock market is like riding a roller coaster, employers have to be more discerning about whom they choose to hire. It's up to you to promote yourself, and to demonstrate the skills you possess and the benefits you'll bring to an organization.

Second, you have to understand your audience. Everyone has different needs, and by assessing those needs, you'll know what qualities from your personal résumé you'll have to access. Your skill bank is the same; it's just a matter of knowing which tools to bring out to fit the situation.

Today I'm a motivational speaker. I lecture about the importance of attitude, behavior, and perform-ance, and it's my aim to show people how to be more productive and happy. What's *your* 60-second sound bite? Write it, learn it, and rehearse it. Always be ready to promote *you*, because you never know when your next big opportunity will come along.

CHAPTER 15

● ● ● ● ● ● ● ● ● ● ● ● ● ●

I've Got Something to Say

"Hope deferred makes the heart sick,
but when dreams come true,
there is life and joy."
— Proverbs 13:12

During my tenure at the Product Center, IBM had a big contest in San Francisco to see which sales rep could best demonstrate a new software program we were selling called "Lotus 1-2-3." None of us knew much about the product—except that it was very intimidating.

I also didn't know that one of my co-workers, Joe Russell, had gone to our store manager, Jody Hughes, with a message: "None of us are very excited about participating in this contest. We should just go ahead and send Keith Harrell to the meeting. He's our best shot—he'll win."

And Jody had agreed.

Since I knew I'd be competing against the best sales reps in the country, I stayed up late for weeks trying to learn all about the program, its unique advantages, and how to make using it

look easy. I kept my strategy simple: It was all about selling—
tieing the features, functions, and benefits back to the customer's needs.

When the date of the meeting arrived, I made my presentation in front of the regional managers, staff, and an instructor
from the IBM sales school in Atlanta. I was in the zone, and I
won the contest and a free trip to Hawaii.

It sounded great until I realized that the "vacation" included working at the local IBM Product Center part of the time. I
didn't have much desire to go on an excursion like that, so I
placed a few calls and came up with a better idea. I traded in the
Hawaii trip for a new Sony console television, which I presented to my mom as a gift.

I returned from San Francisco exhilarated after winning the
contest, yet the feeling wore off as my day-to-day reality continued. Working in a retail environment from 8 A.M. to 5 P.M.
and coming in on Saturdays was a real challenge, since I was
used to a more flexible schedule. But this meant that I was at
the Product Center late one Friday afternoon when I got a
phone call from the human resources department—a call that
would be a turning point in my professional life.

"Keith? Oh, thank goodness you're still there," said the
woman on the other end of the line. I could actually feel the
relief coming through the receiver. "I'm at my wit's end. I think
you're the only person who could possibly help me."

"Okay, just relax," I said, trying to help her calm down.
"What can I do for you?"

"Well, I need someone to speak at a meeting tomorrow. I
know it's very short notice, but I'm stuck."

"What's this meeting about?" I asked, feeling more uneasy
as the conversation unfolded.

"Well, it's a career day for 500 high-achieving minority

high school seniors," she replied. "They're standouts in science and math, and all the top professionals from the Seattle area will be there to talk to them about the importance of those subjects. There will be judges, attorneys, doctors, and businesspeople, all of whom are successful minority men and women themselves. The woman we usually send to functions such as this has been called out of town due to a family emergency. The meeting is tomorrow on the campus of the University of Washington. Will you do it?"

"Isn't there anyone else who can take her place?" I implored. "Maybe you can get someone from the other branch office."

"I've tried the other branches. No luck."

The more I thought about it, the more I wondered, *Why do they want me? I didn't even major in math or science in college.* Then it dawned on me. There were two obvious reasons why I was being called for this task: One, it was Friday—everybody else had probably already gone home or made plans for the weekend; and two, it was a *minority* career day.

I was the perfect man for the job, and I didn't have a good excuse for turning it down, so I said, "Okay, I'll do it." I figured that if nothing else, it might be a good way for me to raise my profile at IBM and in the community.

The next morning when I woke up at 7 A.M., I had no idea what I should speak about, so I called my friend Ralph for some advice. "I need your help," I confessed. "I'm supposed to talk at a career day, and the only reason they chose me is because someone had an emergency and I'm the only black person they could find on such short notice—"

"Keith, slow down," Ralph interrupted. "You can do it."

"But what should I talk about?"

"Speak about attitude and winning in the game of life," he replied.

"How?" I asked.

"Tell them *your* story," Ralph suggested. "Tell them about your athletic career and how you went from hoping to play pro basketball to the disappointment of not getting drafted. Tell them about how you prepared yourself for your job at IBM, and how attitude made the difference."

"Yeah, that sounds good . . . ," I trailed off.

"It *is* good, Keith. It's a good story about winning and losing and setting yourself up after being knocked down. You're always saying 'Attitude is everything,' so talk about that."

By the time I arrived at the University of Washington campus, I was ready. I was so excited about having the opportunity to share my experience that my attitude was making a difference—in *me*.

I discovered that the master of ceremonies for the day was one of my former high school teachers, Mr. Lee. He explained that each speaker would be allotted 25 minutes to talk and another 5 minutes for questions and answers. Since my turn was toward the end of the program, I found a seat at the back of the room.

The speakers that day were an amazing collection of some of Seattle's most prominent citizens. I was so impressed with what each of them had to say that I began taking notes. To my amazement, I appeared to be the only one doing so. Everyone else was just listening to the presentations, and some of the kids appeared to be very bored.

The more I heard, the more excited I became. No one was touching upon the information that I wanted to cover, so I was in a great position to give my speech. I could feel the adrenaline flowing as my moment in the spotlight drew near.

But we were running out of time. The other speakers had exceeded their 25 minutes, so when it was my turn, there wasn't sufficient time to finish. Mr. Lee stood up to announce his plan. "We're almost out of time, and the program states that we have two guest lecturers remaining. So, instead of having them both speak, I'm going to ask them to come forward for questions and answers."

Before I realized what I was doing, I was on my feet. "We can't stop now!" I yelled from the back of the room. "You can't wrap it up, Mr. Lee. I've got some things I want to share!"

My former teacher realized that I was a man on a mission. "It looks as if we've saved our best presentation for last," he told the group.

I strode up to the front of the room and began my speech. "I have something very important I want to impart to you today," I said. "It's about *attitude*." I did exactly what Ralph had suggested earlier that morning: I told the students about winning and losing on and off the basketball court, self-esteem, motivation, and the power of attitude. I spoke for 25 minutes nonstop, and the crowd absolutely loved it. In fact, they gave me a standing ovation.

One woman came up to me after it was over and said, "That was amazing! I thought I was at an Amway convention. I'm convinced—attitude *is* everything!"

I knew something special had happened that day, and I wouldn't forget it. I felt a sense of satisfaction that went beyond the audience's positive feedback . . . I really enjoyed speaking, and I felt that my message had made a difference.

▲ ▲ ▲

My speaking debut led me to make some changes in my own life as well. As with any job, my position at IBM had its ups and downs, but I'd begun to feel trapped. I knew that in order to move up the corporate ladder, I needed to chart a career path. The problem was that I didn't have a clear understanding of my options—that is, until the day that the regional manager, Craig Alhmstrom, flew in from San Francisco to meet with several members of the Product Center staff.

"Keith, let's you and me go for a little walk," Craig said.

"Okay," I replied, knowing that he probably didn't just want to catch a breath of fresh air.

After a little small talk, he turned to me and said, "Keith, you're stagnating. You really have to do something else."

"I appreciate your talking to me," I responded, "but I really don't know what else I want to do in my career."

"What about management?"

"No, that's not for me," I answered. I didn't like all the politics I saw in management, so I wanted no part of it. I was still dealing with issues such as Coby Sillers's decision to rank my performance as a four my first year on quota, the consolidation of my territory the following year, the management neglecting to provide me with any solid systems training, and the way the administrators at the Product Center Store played favorites when it came to distributing leads.

"You need to grow, Keith," Craig continued. "Can I make a suggestion?"

"Sure," I replied.

"They're looking for guest instructors for the retail-sales training school down in Atlanta. We think you'd be great at it."

I looked around as we walked. Part of me thought that being an instructor would be fantastic, but I still doubted that I was smart or technical enough.

"I-I don't know," I stammered.

"Look. Just go down there for two weeks and see what you think of it."

I replied the only way I knew how: "If you make me do it, then I'll do it. And I'll try my hardest to be the best guest instructor they've ever had."

That was good enough for Craig, and the matter was settled.

I spent the next few weeks preparing for my guest position. I practiced, reviewed my material, polished up on teaching techniques, learned the products, and worked on my writing and presentation skills. I was motivated.

When I got to Atlanta, something happened: I loved it! I'd found my passion in teaching. Even better, IBM loved my work, and I received a high rating from the class and the retail staff. Shortly after returning to Seattle, I started to hear talk that management was considering promoting me to Atlanta.

For the first time in my eight years at IBM, I finally had a vision of a job I wanted. I thought I'd always have to be in sales because I didn't want a managerial position, but now I knew that my true calling was to be an *instructor*. Maybe it was the influence of my dad and my uncle teaching at the college level all those years—the profession was in my genes.

I went back to Seattle and told my store manager what I wanted to do. He was excited for me and gave me some important advice: "You have to get your numbers up; otherwise you won't get promoted to instructor."

I was familiar with the store politics of giving the leads to certain sales reps, and I knew that the practice affected the numbers, but that factor was out of my control. So I decided I'd work my hardest; that was all I could do.

Six months passed, and a new store manager was installed at the Product Center. I was still waiting to hear from Atlanta. Two more months went by, and finally, the new manager called me in to his office. "You haven't been performing your best, and your numbers aren't where they should be. You just don't seem to be giving it your all. I'm putting you on a program, and then we'll evaluate you in 90 days. If your numbers aren't up, I'll have to let you go."

I was shocked. I'd never been cut before in my life! I thought he'd called me in to *promote* me; I'd never been in a position where anybody was going to *fire* me. I was devastated but tried to maintain my composure. I bit my lip as I felt the tears welling up in my eyes.

I took a deep breath. Choosing my words very carefully, I said, "I've been waiting for months to hear from management about when I'd be promoted to sales instructor. I can't believe you're talking about putting me on a program."

"I didn't know anything about a promotion or your wanting to be an instructor," he said to my surprise.

"They didn't tell you?" I asked, incredulously.

"No. This is the first time I've heard anything about it. So how about if we start all over?"

"Okay," I replied. But I was really thinking, *Who can I trust?* Now I was more determined than ever to achieve my dream of working in Atlanta.

▲ ▲ ▲

LESSON 15:
Play with *Your* NBA
▲ ▲ ▲ ▲ ▲ ▲ ▲ ▲ ▲

I can't count the number of times I've been asked if I play with the NBA (the fact that I stand a little over 6'6" tall may have something to do with the inquiry). When asked, I always respond with a resounding yes. Naturally, the next question is, "What position?" I tell people I play all positions: I'm the guard, forward, and center; I'm the player, coach, and general manager;

and I'm also the leading scorer and most valuable player. You see, I play with my **N**atural **B**orn **A**bilities, and I'm slam-dunking every day!

God has given each of us talents. He's equipped us with everything we need to fulfill our purpose. Some of us have the gift to teach and speak, as I do. Some of us are great leaders and managers. Some people can organize anything from their kitchen drawer to a 10,000-person conference, while some are called to serve others as missionaries and non-profit volunteers. We all have gifts, and when we identify, develop, excel, and work with our natural-born abilities, we find purpose, passion, success, and joy in life.

In order to maximize your talents, you must remember one key concept: *Attitude Is Everything!* I've researched, developed, and professed this idea ever since that Saturday morning at the University of Washington when I spoke to those students. Your attitude is reflected in your behavior, which ultimately impacts your success. The good thing about attitude is that everyone has one, and it's up to each of us whether we'll have a positive or negative one. You must decide whether your attitude will propel you to success or plummet you to failure.

It doesn't matter whether you're in the mail room or the boardroom, if you're the secretary or the CEO, what matters is how you use your abilities and your attitude. Maximizing your NBA and maintaining a positive attitude is the formula that will have you "slam-dunking" in life!

CHAPTER 16

· · · · · · · · · · · · · ·

Whatever It Takes

*"Work hard and cheerfully at
whatever you do, as though you
were working for the Lord
rather than for people."*
— Colossians 3:23

Three days after my meeting with the store manager, a memo was circulated: "IBM has sold its Product Centers to a company called NYNEX." My dream of going to Atlanta was over.

There was an offer on the table of $5,000 for anyone who would stay on to work for NYNEX, while the employees who wanted to remain with IBM would have to attend two years' worth of large-account mainframe and systems training. The decision was complicated: I didn't want to sever my ties with IBM, but going back through training wasn't going to be easy. To make matters worse, the people in the other divisions didn't have the most favorable impression of those of us in the Office Products Division—our initials were OPD, so the derogatory nickname around the rest of the company was "Opey-Dopey." Needless to say, the thought of working with people who might belittle me was discouraging at best.

Training was intense and would consist of 18 months in a branch office and 6 months in Atlanta and Dallas. Since IBM was consolidating, I'd be trained with other people from all divisions of the company—I might be sitting next to a computer-chip designer or a Harvard MBA, but if I couldn't compete with my fellow employees, I'd be let go. It was all part of the company's redeployment strategy.

As if this wasn't enough, I had problems in my personal life as well. For three months I'd dated a wonderful young lady, and I felt that we had become really good friends. It caught me off guard when she announced that she didn't want to see me anymore. I was reeling.

My cousin Kenny heard about my string of misfortunes and dropped by the Product Center Store one day to see me. "I've got just the thing for you," he said.

"What is it?" I asked.

"I think you'd benefit from taking a course I just took called "The Pursuit of Excellence." It will help you get refocused and regain your confidence."

Kenny was correct—I took the class and loved it. In addition, I took a life-changing class called "Increasing Human Effectiveness," taught by Bob Moawad of Edge Learning Institute in Tacoma, Washington. The two-and-a-half-day seminar explored the importance of personal accountability, self-awareness, and attitude. I learned how to plot a course of action for my life and focus on the future and the positive things that were in store for me. It taught me everything, and I came out of it totally reenergized. *I've got plenty of opportunities out there right now,* I thought. Now I knew what I wanted to do. Of the

12 people who had worked at the IBM Product Center Store, only 2 ended up staying with IBM. I was one of them, and I completely dedicated myself to training.

My first class was very thorough. There were people from every division within the company, and, as I'd anticipated, most of them were very talented and bright. But I refused to be intimidated, and I ended up doing very well. Of course, that was only the first in a series of six classes that I needed to complete my training.

It was at about this time that I heard IBM was looking for instructors to help teach some marketing classes. Because of my background at the company (including eight years in sales), I thought I'd be qualified to teach some of the basic selling classes. Plus, as a guest instructor at the retail-sales training school, I had already demonstrated that I had good teaching skills. The more I investigated the opportunity, the more interested I became. I was told, "You need to get approval from your branch manager to pursue the position," so I went back and talked it over with him.

"It's only a two-year assignment. It sounds like a dead-end kind of job to me," was his summation. "What's your goal after that?"

"I don't know," I replied in all honesty. "It took me eight years to get *this* two-year plan."

"Well, you need to be working on a five-year plan. If you don't have a goal after your two-year position, then you really don't have a strategy. So, with that in mind, I'm not going to send you down to Atlanta to apply for that job—not now, not ever."

I was discouraged, but I held on to my dream. *Someday I'm going to be an IBM instructor,* I told myself. I continued to go through the training, applying everything I'd learned from the self-help course and my athletic career. I also began to network—I met with people who knew more than I did about certain aspects of the business so that we could work together. In turn, I'd assist them in the areas that I had experience in.

Even more important, I began to develop a new routine during the training sessions: I started giving brief motivational talks in class. The instructor would bring me up to the front of the room at different times, like right after a difficult exam, and say, "Keith, can you give us a positive word?"

I'd launch into a speech that would encourage and motivate my classmates. I came to the realization that people are hungry for positive messages, and I began calling my presentations "Attitude Is Everything."

Amazingly enough, I had no problem coming up with material. A short time before this, someone had sent me a copy of Zig Ziglar's book *See You at the Top*. I took that book and my *Unlocking Your Potential* affirmations, which I'd gotten from the "Increasing Human Effectiveness" class, with me when I went off to IBM training. I read Zig's book and the affirmations faithfully, memorizing portions of each and later using them as the basis for my inspirational speeches in class.

The final training class was called "IBM Sales School." On the second day of the class, the instructor asked for nominations for class officers. Since I was motivated to learn from every possible experience, I immediately raised my hand and nominated myself. The instructor acknowledged me, and I jumped up from my seat and enthusiastically explained to the class why I should be president. I went into my background, experience, sales training—everything I could think of that would qualify me for leadership.

I guess the class liked what they heard, because I was elected president. People could see my passion and sense that I was really sincere. For many of us, getting to the final course had been a tremendous challenge, and in my campaign speech I expressed my appreciation for the help I'd received from my fellow students. Because of them, I'd made it this far, and as class president, I guaranteed them that I'd be a leader . . . and someone they could trust.

I loved selling, so the last class was my favorite. One of our assignments was to make six sales calls. If we made a sale, the instructor would reward us—we might be recognized in front of the class or given a small gift as an acknowledgment of our salesmanship. I was excited about what was going on in this class; it motivated me in a big way.

I did extremely well in the course and scored very high on the exams. At the conclusion of "Sales School," I was inducted into the Hall of Fame, which represented the top one percent of everyone who had *ever* gone through the sales training at IBM. I was pumped up.

Yet past patterns resurfaced when I was assigned a sales territory that no one else wanted. I thought I'd already proven to everyone that I could sell—based on the results of sales school, I was one of the best—but there I was in a dead-end territory, going nowhere. No matter how often I pleaded my case to my marketing manager, it seemed that he'd just drag his feet. So, once again, I was facing impossible odds—I wasn't going to make my numbers. Several co-workers even went to my manager and told him how close I was, but to no avail. I didn't make quota.

I needed to get away. I wanted some quiet time alone to clear my head, meditate, and pray. I went to Europe, and it was a good break for me. I came back determined to make the 100% Club the next year.

There were several different managers to whom I reported after I'd completed systems training. When I returned from Europe, I was finally working for a person who seemed to notice the unfair treatment directed toward me, and he decided to do his own investigation.

He went to the branch manager on my behalf and asked a lot of questions, and the answers he received shocked him. He came back from that meeting and called me into his office.

"I could lose my job for what I'm about to do," he began.

"What's going on?" I asked.

"I've got to ask you some questions, Keith," he continued. "Some of them may sound stupid, but I need to ask them, okay?"

"Okay," I agreed, still having no idea where all this was leading.

"Keith, do you drive a Mercedes?"

"Yes."

"Did you just go to Europe?"

"Yes."

"Did you just build yourself a house?"

"Yes," I replied, wondering where he was going with this.

The manager paused, swallowed hard, and asked one last question: *"Keith, do you sell drugs?"*

"NO!" I blurted out. "I don't sell drugs, and I don't use them, either!"

I was shocked. I'd suspected there was a reason that I was being set up for failure time and time again, but now I knew that I was being discriminated against.

We sat there in silence for a moment until I broached the obvious question: "Why would you even ask me that?"

My manager leaned over his desk. "I just talked to the folks upstairs, and they can't figure how you've been able to do some of the things you've been doing. All they can conclude is that you're somehow mixed up in drugs."

Race clearly played a role in this accusation, and I tried my best to remain calm. "Okay, let me see if I can explain some things," I said. "First, let's talk about my car. I have several friends in Europe. When I learned that the dollar was very strong compared to the gilder—three to one—I made contact with a European Mercedes-Benz dealer and imported three cars, which I presold. This enabled me to purchase a fourth car for myself at a significantly reduced price.

"Concerning my house: When I was going through training last year, I sold my car and used that money as a down payment on a lot so I could one day build a house. Do you know who I bought the lot from?"

He shook his head.

"My *grandmother*," I replied. "I put a down payment on my grandmother's land so I could build a house."

"I see," he said.

"And the trip to Europe was a special deal through Continental Airlines—using all the frequent-flyer miles I'd accumulated while I was going through various training programs in Atlanta and Dallas over the past eight years."

Sheepishly, my manager asked if it would be all right for him to pass this information up the chain of command. "No problem," I responded. "I have nothing to hide—take it up there. Tell the branch manager, the regional manager, and anybody else you have to tell to get it right," I firmly stated.

So he did just that, and everyone was embarrassed. The light of understanding was beginning to dawn: I hadn't been going anywhere at IBM because they thought I was selling drugs. Once that issue was cleared up, things started moving in a more positive direction.

Once again, I was given a new manager. Craig Kairis was

now my boss, and I knew this was a good thing. I'd trained Craig back in Office Products, and we'd remained good friends over the years.

Actually, Craig had wanted a management position for several years, but the politics of IBM up to that point had worked against him as well. Those higher up on the food chain had based their decisions on the fact that guys such as him and me were from the lowest echelon of IBMers . . . we were Opey-Dopeys.

But Craig finally landed a management position. As my new boss, one of the first things he said to me was, "Keith, this management team doesn't know who you are. They don't recognize your potential. If you trust me, I believe I can get you promoted out of here to the job you really want as a training instructor. It won't be easy, and it may take some time. Are you with me on this?"

"You bet I am, Craig," I replied enthusiastically. "Thanks." *I trained him well,* I thought.

Craig and I began to map out a strategic plan to realize my goal of becoming a training instructor. He was in charge of a major IBM product announcement that all the employees in the region were to attend—the new product was the AS/400 computer system. It was replacing two of the most successful computer systems in IBM's history: the System/36 and System/38. "I want you to go to Dallas for one week, learn all you can about this product, and then come back and tell us all about it in a 25-minute presentation at the regional meeting."

"Craig, I-I don't know . . . " I stammered, suddenly unsure of myself.

"I believe in you," Craig said confidently. "I know you can do it. How badly do you want to go to Atlanta and be an instructor? The management team needs to see you in action, and there's no better opportunity than this one."

So I went to Dallas, learned all I could, and came back prepared to make the presentation. The day of the product announcement, the ballroom at the Seattle Sheraton hotel was filled with more than 1,000 IBM employees. When I arrived, I was told that there were four of us on the program and that I'd be speaking third. I listened as attentively as I could to the first two presenters and waited my turn.

When it was time, I stood up, took a deep breath, and jumped into my presentation with the fervor of a Pentecostal preacher. My excitement was contagious—the level of intensity and enthusiasm in the room shot off the chart. If you'd been standing outside, you'd have sworn there was a spiritual revival going on. I had them dancing in the aisles, singing and shouting *"Hallelujah!"*

Ironically, the one person who wasn't in attendance at that meeting was my branch manager—the one who'd told me that going to sales training to become an instructor was basically a dead-end job. He was on vacation at the time, but when he returned, there was a message waiting for him from *his* boss: "Who is Keith Harrell, and why isn't he conducting every product introduction meeting and teaching others how to do it?"

I was getting invitations from managers around the region to do program events. I made my sales quota, thanks in large part to Craig and the support he gave me—I'd never received such backing from anyone else at IBM before. So all was in place for the move to Atlanta.

In a "managers only" meeting right before the end of the year, someone mentioned me as a candidate for promotion. My branch manager said, "I think Keith should do one more year here in the branch office working with a large account team before we promote him." But he was challenged by every other manager in attendance. "Not one more year—*this year*," they said in unison.

So I went to Atlanta and interviewed with three people for the job opening as a sales-school instructor. The interviews went well, and I got the job. I was a training instructor, and it was great!

I knew for the first time in my career that I wouldn't be controlled by a quota or given a bad territory. I'd now be evaluated and measured by the students in my classroom based on my ability to educate and motivate them. I loved teaching, and it showed: In my second year, I was voted the number-one instructor in Marketing Education, thanks, in part, to some special people in my life who really motivated me—people such as Karen Hardy, Diane Andrews, Pam Keith, and Kathy Sequerth.

As my third year wound down, IBM announced that they were forming a company called "Skill Dynamics" to take over the training division of IBM. At the time, I didn't think about the change all that much, but it would quickly affect my career in a big way.

Bob Bradshaw became my new manager. He called me into his office one day to ask me a question: "I hear you have your own business. Is that true?"

"Yes, it is," I answered. People had begun to ask me to make presentations outside of IBM, so I'd started my own speaking business on the side. It was very small, but I was quite proud of it.

"What's your business called?" Bob asked.

"Harrell and Associates," I replied.

"Who are your associates?"

"There's only one—my mom."

"Well, that doesn't sound very promising to me," Bob said sarcastically. "Plus, this creates a bit of a problem."

"Problem?" I inquired.

"Yes. Now that we've become Skill Dynamics, we'd like to

create some new revenue opportunities for the company. One way to do that is to sell your motivational speeches to our customers. Since you work for us, having your own company creates a conflict of interest."

"I don't really see it that way," I said. I began to explain why I thought we were completely separate from each other, but Bob wasn't interested in hearing it.

"You're going to have to make a decision, Keith," he said. "You either stay with us and shut down your own company, or else you'll have to leave."

"Are you asking me to fire my mother? I can't do that."

He replied, "How many customers do you have?"

"One, but we're going to grow."

He laughed. "It's your decision."

It didn't take long for me to make up my mind. I just couldn't walk away from the work I loved—work that gave me a sense of purpose. For the first time in my career, I believed I was making a difference. I'd dreamed of this opportunity, and I wasn't about to give up on my dream.

So I left the newly formed Skill Dynamics. And I never looked back.

I turned the second bedroom of my home into an office, and I started calling all sorts of people, asking them if they'd hire me to speak. I'd already booked my first paid engagement some five months earlier, and it happened to be scheduled for the very day I officially started my solo operation. That morning I didn't need any alarm clock to wake me up—the president and CEO of Harrell and Associates had things to do. After delivering my speech, I remember the realization hitting me like a ton of bricks: *You have no more IBM to go back to. You're on your own now.*

My first breakthrough was making contact with several local school districts. I was able to convince the superintendents that my speech, *Attitude Is Everything,* was vital for teachers to hear because of the tremendous impact they have on students. In turn, they ran it by their school boards, and it won approval.

Another early client of mine was the state of Georgia. I'd launched a grassroots effort—making dozens of phone calls from my office—and, as a result, I was invited to speak to several government agencies about the importance of attitude in public service.

God's grace was evident in the entire process. IBM managers were still interested in hiring me, and, thankfully, when they called my former colleagues, they were given my home number to contact me. One regional manager booked me nine times in the first six months. IBM still calls me for bookings, and to this day I'm very grateful to them for helping me develop my God-given talent. I'm still very loyal . . . you cut me and I bleed "blue."

The transition from IBM training instructor to professional speaker was challenging, to say the least, and not everyone was as sure as I was that I'd make it on my own. My dad had spent his entire career at the same community college, and he believed in job security, loyalty, and sticking with a situation through thick and thin. In his estimation, I was a young man with financial obligations and a new career that was low on clientele. It wasn't surprising that he had some questions for me upon hearing the news of my career change.

"How do people hire you?" he asked.

"They call me up," I replied.

"How many people have called so far?"

I was hoping he wouldn't ask that. "None," I answered.

"How are they going to find out about you to hire you?" he

questioned.

"I'm going to do a mass mailing and some telemarketing. I'm going to use all the sales techniques that I learned at IBM. The only difference now is that the product is *me*."

"Hmm . . . ," he mused.

"It'll work, Dad, I just know it will," I assured him.

"Son, it's not going to be easy. Do you have a contingency plan if this speaking thing doesn't work out? Let me ask you this: Are you prepared to get a roommate?"

"Whatever it takes, Dad."

"Rent out the house and move into an apartment?"

"Whatever it takes, Dad."

"Get a second job, sell your car, and move home with your mother?"

"Dad, if I have to move back home, live in the basement, and sleep on a cot, then that's what I'm prepared to do. I'm going to make it on my own, and what I'm doing right now is what I'm supposed to be doing."

It was at this point that he ceased his questions. I couldn't quite figure out why he wasn't talking—he seemed to be weighing all my arguments in his mind, getting ready to pronounce his final judgment. I'll never forget what he said next: "Keith, you've convinced me. Son, you've got W-I-T."

"W-I-T? What are you talking about, Dad?"

"You've got a _Whatever It Takes_ attitude—W-I-T. And that's what it's going to take for you to make it out there on your own."

So with my parents on my team and a Whatever It Takes attitude, I launched my new career.

LESSON 16:
Changing Challenges to Opportunities
▲ ▲ ▲ ▲ ▲ ▲ ▲ ▲ ▲

Anticipating and handling change can be difficult. When change seems threatening or overwhelming, you need to reframe it as an opportunity to learn, try something different, and reevaluate goals and objectives. Recognize that true change often takes time; generally it's a gradual process, so be patient with yourself.

In my case, every time IBM made a change, I was presented with a new challenge. I faced those challenges head-on, evolving from a sales rep to an instructor along the way. But sometimes the best way to make a major leap in life is to let go and strive for something better: Ultimately, I realized that I had to let go of IBM in order to actualize my dream of owning my own business.

Because of my experience at IBM, I'm prepared and equipped to deal with the ever-changing needs and challenges in my business today. I've learned to not only accept change but also to anticipate and look forward to it, because without change there is no growth. As Dr. Martin Luther King, Jr., said, "The ultimate measure of a man is not where he stands in moments of comfort and convenience, but where he stands at times of challenge and controversy." Be thankful for change and the challenges it creates— they force you out of your comfort zone, teach you about yourself, and help you evaluate what's most important to you.

A few affirmations can help you maintain a positive attitude during times of turmoil. Post them, speak them, believe them, and turn the challenges of change into opportunities for positive growth:

- I accept the reality of this change, and I intend to convert this "threat" into an opportunity.

- I acknowledge that change is an essential part of life.

- I will take this change one step at a time to keep it manageable.

- I will not put off meeting the challenges of this change.

- I will do whatever it takes to master this change and create balance in my life.

- I will celebrate each small step through this change process, and I will practice gratitude for the blessings I've received.

CHAPTER 17

Walking by Faith

"The righteous will live by faith."
— Romans 1:17

Two weeks before I left IBM's Skill Dynamics, I went to see a co-worker, David Peoples. I'd always respected Dave, and I knew that as a top speaker and instructor, he'd give me the straight scoop on the field I was entering into.

"I've decided to go out on my own as a professional speaker," I told him. "I'm pretty sure that this is what I should be doing. Do you have any words of wisdom to pass on to me?"

Dave smiled. "First of all, congratulations. I know you have the potential to be a good speaker. But, if you don't mind, I do have a suggestion that I think will be very valuable to you."

"Sure. Tell me what you have in mind."

Dave told me, "You should really consider attending the National Speakers Association's (NSA) annual convention. This year they're holding it in Orlando, Florida. If I were you, I'd make sure that I joined the association and attended their meetings."

"Okay . . . ," I replied, slowly considering his advice.

"I think this event will give you the *confirmation* you're looking for."

That was exactly what I needed to hear. I joined the NSA, signed up for the conference, and three weeks later I was on my way to Orlando.

When I arrived in the hotel lobby, the first thing that caught my eye was a group of people all dressed up in their Sunday best. Having gotten over my shyness years ago, I went up to one of the ladies and asked her what group they were with.

"We're here attending the annual African Methodist Episcopal Church convention," she replied kindly.

"Well, isn't that something!" I exclaimed. "When I was growing up, I attended First AME Church in Seattle."

"Is that right?"

"Yes," I continued. "And I remember that our pastor, the Rev. Adams, always gave the most powerful and effective sermons. Is he going to be here by any chance?"

"Rev. Adams?" She thought for a moment. "Oh, you must mean *Bishop* John Hurst Adams. Yes, he most definitely will be here this week."

"Come to think of it, there was one other minister I knew during my college years who had a big impact on me. Do you know if the Reverend Cecil Murray will be in attendance?"

"Yes, Rev. Murray will be here, too."

I thanked the woman for her time and information, and I moved on toward the registration table for the NSA convention. *What an amazing coincidence that the AME meeting is also here!* I thought. But I was about to understand that this was more than a mere accident—God was at work. He was confirming my decision.

The next day I went to the hotel ballroom for the first session of the conference. I checked the program to see who the opening speaker would be, and my eyes nearly popped out of my head when I read the name: *Og Mandino*. My mind raced back to that summer before my senior year in high school when Lindsey Stuart, the director of the Rotary Boys' Club, would read us the passage from Og Mandino's book *The Greatest Salesman in the World*. I remembered all the hard work my teammates and I had put in to becoming the high school state champions. *Maybe Og's being here is a reminder that it will take a lot of effort, but I can achieve my goal,* I thought. I almost couldn't believe that I was in the same hotel as he was—not to mention Bishop Adams and Rev. Murray. Confirmation was coming through loud and clear. But there were still more surprises in store for me at the convention. . . .

About a year before I left IBM, I was invited to give a sales-training session for the loan executives at the Seattle United Way chapter. After I finished, a woman invited me to speak to a group at the Washington Parks and Recreation Conference in nearby Bellevue. So I took a vacation day from IBM in Atlanta, flew back to Washington, and delivered my talk. It was a big deal for me, since it was the first freelance job I'd ever done. That night I couldn't sleep because I was still wound up after giving my speech, so I turned on the TV and started surfing through the channels. I landed on one of those late-night infomercials, and the featured speaker was Tony Robbins. I was intrigued by one of the concepts he presented: "If you're trying to achieve something, follow behind someone who's already doing it. Get a plan and a strategy." I realized that I needed a mentor or coach to help me out.

Back in Atlanta the next week, I went to see Dr. Ed Metcalf, or "Dr. Ed," as he preferred to be called. He was one of the top trainers at IBM and practically a legend in the world of speaking, so, given his reputation, it was a bit intimidating to knock on his door and ask for advice. But that's precisely what I did.

"Good morning, Dr. Ed," I said. "My name is Keith Harrell, and I work here. The reason I'm coming to see you today is because I want to be just like you."

"Well, that's impossible," he replied.

I was puzzled by his response. "Why?"

"Because you're 6'6" and black, and I'm 5'11" and white," he joked with a broad smile on his face. "That's why."

I couldn't help but smile back at him. "I want to go out and *speak* all over the world, just like you do," I clarified, hoping that he'd say more.

He did. "I'll tell you what I can do, Keith. I'll pass your name on to some of the people who have hired me to speak at the IBM User Group conferences. I'll do whatever I can to help you."

"That's exactly what I was hoping you'd say. I recently saw an infomercial with Tony Robbins, and it spurred me on to ask for your help," I explained.

So as I sat in the ballroom of the Peabody Orlando Hotel, looking over the NSA's program of events, I was provided yet another confirmation when I saw that the conference's closing session would feature none other than . . . Tony Robbins.

▲ ▲ ▲

The contacts I made at the NSA convention were positive and helpful. I met a lady named Juanell Teague, a consultant who helps people transition into speaking careers. She teaches a course called "Focus or Die," and she really helped me fine-tune my approach and realize that my core message should center on attitude, change, and performance.

There were many people at the conference who came up to me and asked, "What do you speak on?"

I'd answer, "I'm a motivational speaker," and they'd cluck their tongues.

"The industry isn't looking for a lot of motivational speakers anymore because it's just a lot of fluff," said my detractors.

That was news to me. I knew that IBM hired motivational speakers, and they seemed to meet a real need. When I met Hattie Hill and Thelma Wells later on, they reminded me of the 10-Percent Rule: "Many people in this industry will tell you a lot of stuff that sounds great—but don't believe everything you hear," they advised. "Your job is to focus on the 10 percent that feels right for you. Forget 90 percent of what's said, because most of the time only 10 percent applies to your particular situation."

Motivational speaking was what I wanted to do, and I left that convention determined to do it. On the plane flying home, I sat back in my seat and thought, *Dave Peoples was right. This conference gave me the confirmation that I needed. Now I know that this is what God wants me to do.*

▲ ▲ ▲

LESSON 17:
Confirmation to Conviction
▲ ▲ ▲ ▲ ▲ ▲ ▲ ▲ ▲

When I joined IBM, it was one of the best sales companies in the world. But during my 14-year tenure, I watched the company lose market share, and, for the first time in their history, lay off employees. Things had changed at Big Blue, and it was time for me to follow my dream of becoming a successful entrepreneur.

I'd already allowed fear to keep me from pursuing my childhood aspiration of playing pro ball, so I wasn't about to walk away from my fledgling speaking business when Bob Bradshaw presented me with his ultimatum. I'd known for a while that I needed to leave Skill Dynamics, but I hadn't been convinced that I could make it on my own. After all, it requires a leap of faith to leave a known for an unknown—even when you're sure that what you're doing is right.

I stepped out with nothing but my faith to guide me, and I was looking for a sign that I was making the right move. The NSA annual convention was my confirmation; the people I met and the messages they delivered solidified my beliefs and erased my doubts. When I returned home, I discussed my decision to resign with my dad and a few trusted colleagues, and I had several long talks with God. Through reading and meditating on His word and lots of prayer, I knew in my heart that I was making the right choice. My affirmation led to firm conviction, and today I'm a very successful motivational speaker.

I had no way of knowing how things would turn out, but God did—and He sent me more than one sign. When you're pursuing your dream, and it's in step with God's plan for your life, He will send you the confirmation you need to pursue your passion.

CHAPTER 18

Early Mistakes,
Early Lessons

*"Now glory be to God! By his mighty
power at work within us, he is able to
accomplish infinitely more than we
would ever dare to ask or hope."*
— Ephesians 3:20

The biggest mistake I made early on in my career as a speaker was thinking that I was better than I really was. I left IBM as a top sales instructor, so I was sure that the transition into the speaking business would be easy . . . but I was wrong.

I tried to make some connections through speakers' bureaus—agencies that contract lecturers for corporate and association meetings and conferences. I found the phone number of Jordan International Enterprises, a speakers' bureau in Atlanta headed by Dupree Jordan, and decided to give them a call.

"Do you have a videotape of your work?" Dupree asked after we'd exchanged small talk for a few minutes.

"Well . . . ," I replied, hesitating. I didn't have one prepared, but I decided to improvise. "Actually, I *do* have a video of myself speaking to an IBM audience, but the quality isn't that great."

"Send it to me," he said. "I just want to see your speaking style. The quality of the tape won't matter at this point."

"Okay, I'll send it today!"

But Dupree Jordan didn't call me back. So I phoned him again, this time to find out what he thought of my presentation and how soon it might be before he started booking me. It never even occurred to me that he had *hundreds* of professional speakers at his disposal, as well as many potential lecturers waiting in the wings.

"I looked at your tape," he said, to my pleasant surprise.

"What did you think?" I asked enthusiastically.

"Well, your first two jokes aren't even yours," he critiqued. "I've heard them a hundred times. Here's a good rule to follow: Don't use other people's material—it's not professional."

"Okay," I replied, feeling stung.

"You've got a lot to learn, but you do have potential," he went on to say. "I'm having a speakers' showcase in a few weeks. If you're interested, I can schedule an appointment for you."

At a showcase, meeting planners are invited to see speakers deliver 15 to 30 minutes of their speeches. If any of them have what the planner is looking for, it can lead to bookings. I just knew this was my big opportunity. *I can't wait for everyone to see my presentation style and hear my message,* I thought confidently. *They're going to love me.*

When the day of the showcase arrived, I put on one of my best suits, drove to the location in downtown Atlanta, checked out the stage, and tried to look like a seasoned veteran despite my jitters. I watched several other people give their presentations, and when my turn finally arrived, I hopped up onstage and began yelling and screaming and jumping around as if I were possessed. When I finished, I sat down and thought, *I was the best speaker at the whole showcase!*

So it was particularly disturbing when *no one* called to book me as a result of that event. No one from Jordan Dupree International Enterprises even contacted me. I'd tried to convey my enthusiasm and excitement, but looking back, I realized I was *too* excited. The audience didn't know what to think of me. I found out I had a lot to learn about the business of professional speaking.

I needed to change and grow, and I needed some help. I decided to seek out professionals who could help me hone my skills. By networking with others, I started to understand what it takes to make it in the business of public speaking.

One my first teachers was a gentleman named Larry Winget, whom I'd met in Orlando at the NSA annual convention. I knew that Larry was bright, creative, and an extremely successful speaker, so I was pretty excited when I discovered that he was coming to Atlanta to speak to members of the local NSA group. I picked up the phone, called the president of our chapter, and volunteered to pick Larry up from the airport.

During the drive from the airport to his hotel, I picked Larry's brain. I learned more in the short time I spent with him than I had in the past few months. He knew all about marketing, selling, and the speaking industry. He was the total package, and he shared his insight on everything—from buying a phone system to writing books. (In fact, Larry motivated me to write my first book, *Attitude Is Everything*.)

Another one of the speakers I wanted to learn from was Les Brown. I'd listened to many of his speeches on tape, and I just knew he could give me advice that would be helpful. I phoned his office many times and got to know his assistant, Sue Burkhart, on a first-name basis—but I could never get through to Les directly.

After several months of phone calls, I learned that Les was scheduled to speak at a hotel in Atlanta. That morning I was up and dressed at 6 A.M., even though I knew his talk wouldn't start until 11. I drove down to the hotel and hung out in the lobby, hoping and praying that I might run into him before his speech.

Sure enough, at about 10 A.M., a well-dressed man with a million-dollar smile walked out of an elevator into the lobby. I made eye contact with him and said, "Good morning. How are you doing?"

"Better than good, better than most," he responded cheerfully.

"You must be Les Brown," I said.

"Yes, I am." He smiled even bigger.

"Well, my name is Keith Harrell, and I want you to know that I'm just starting out in the world of professional speaking. I love the way you speak, and I was hoping to get a chance to meet you."

Les was very receptive. He said he'd be delighted to review my demo tape, and he even invited me to sit next to him in the first row while he was being introduced to the audience. During his talk, I kept thinking about the tremendous talents he possessed: He was dynamic and had a great sense of humor and an infectious laugh. Best of all, he told wonderful stories of overcoming his own personal adversity. He made a strong impression on me.

But as I drove home, I began talking to myself in a very negative way: "You aren't right for this kind of work, Keith. You don't have the presentation style or unique background Les has. You don't have his trademark laugh."

Fortunately, when I read my Bible a few days later, I realized that I do have a special gift. I understood that I needed to develop *my* gift and not compare myself with others. I was determined to focus on what God's word says about who I am, and what I'm capable of doing.

By the way, Les did review my demo, and he called me about it one night at 11:30.

"Hello, Keith, it's Les Brown. I just got a chance to take a look at your video," he said.

"What did you think?" I asked.

"Well, the quality of the tape is so poor that I can *hear* you, but I can't *see* you. We need to work on getting you a better demo. You have potential; don't ever forget that."

I didn't.

One of the most important lessons I learned in those early days of my new career was the concept of *taking responsibility*. There may have been people who were willing to help me along the way, but nobody else was going to see to it that I was a success in the world of professional speaking. If it was going to happen, it was going to be because *I* took charge.

The day I printed up my own business cards, my vision became clearer: *Harrell and Associates, Keith Harrell, President/CEO*. I could see my life changing. My hopes were high.

▲ ▲ ▲

My career took off, and I no longer had to worry about not having enough work. In fact, I was working too much. I reached a point where I lost sight of a very important concept: balance.

I started to notice that my legs were swelling up when I was out on the road. I'd been working out with a personal trainer, so at first I assumed it was muscle. I thought, *Hey, this is really good*, because I'd always had fairly thin legs. But it quickly became apparent that something wasn't right. From my knee down to my ankle, my legs were growing larger, especially my left leg. In addition, I was experiencing some pain when I walked. *It's just a pinched nerve*, I tried to convince myself.

"You should go to a chiropractor," one of my friends suggested.

So I did. I got my back adjusted, but my legs were still swollen and the pain was getting worse.

I lived like that for several months. Finally, a few hours before I was scheduled to fly to Los Angeles for a speaking engagement, I stopped by my doctor's office and asked him to examine me. Dr. Rogers came into the exam room, took one look at my legs, and said to me in a very serious voice, "I want you to go see a specialist at the hospital."

I didn't argue. I drove to the hospital and had the specialist look me over. He took some sort of radar-scanning machine and ran it up and down my legs. Once he was finished with the test, he looked at me but didn't say anything. Instead, he picked up the phone and called my doctor.

"Dr. Rogers? Your patient has blood clots in both legs," the specialist announced. Then he handed me the receiver.

I took the phone and tried to sound upbeat, "Hey, Dr. Rogers, I hear I have blood clots. Well, give me whatever prescription I need because I'm on my way to the airport. I'm flying to L.A. to speak to a group of people at Mattel."

"Keith, you can't go," he answered.

"Dr. Rogers, you don't understand. Maybe you haven't heard, but I left IBM awhile ago, and now I'm working for myself. When someone books me, I've got to honor it. It's how I get paid."

There was silence on the other end. Dr. Rogers seemed to be gathering his thoughts. He replied in a tone that went from serious to downright stern. "Keith, I understand what you're saying, but I don't think *you* understand what *I'm* saying. If you were to move too quickly right now, and one of those blood clots released and traveled to your heart or your brain . . . you'd be dead."

All I could say was, "I understand you now."

"Good. So, what I want you to do is get up very slowly, go to your house, get your things, and meet me at the hospital. I'm checking you in immediately. We'll put you on a blood thinner, and you'll probably be on your back for two weeks. Remember, don't move quickly—walk very slowly."

I got off the exam table and began to walk out of the hospital. You've never seen someone walk so slowly in all your life. A woman who had to be 90 years old went speeding past me—that's how deliberately I was moving. I think she felt sorry for me, because after she passed, she turned back and asked, "Do you need me to give you a hand?"

"No, I need more than a hand," I replied. "I need God right now. I've been diagnosed with blood clots."

"Well, I'll pray for you."

"Thank you very much, ma'am."

I drove home, got my stuff, returned to the hospital, and checked in. I called my family to let them know what was going on. My mom offered to fly to Atlanta, but I said, "Mom, don't worry about it. I'm going to be okay."

Then a nurse entered the room. "Mr. Harrell, we need to check your vital signs."

That's when it hit me: *Vital signs? I guess this is really a do-or-die situation.* The nurse checked my pulse, listened to my heart, took my temperature, and took an x-ray.

God was watching over me. He enabled the doctors to find those blood clots in time, and on a beautiful spring day two weeks later, I was released from the hospital in good health.

After being stuck indoors for so long, I was ecstatic to get outside. I thanked the Lord for His blessings and for watching over me. There's no question in my mind that God kept those blood clots from releasing during those months I was neglecting my body.

I've since learned that people who fly a great deal are prone to getting blood clots, so I've developed a strategy for staying healthy on the road. Now I get out of my seat on the airplane and walk around; and I make sure I fly first class, or at least get the extended exit-row seats in coach. It's all about keeping the blood flowing. I don't ever want to take my eye off the ball again.

▲ ▲ ▲

LESSON 18:
When Lost, Ask for Directions
▲ ▲ ▲ ▲ ▲ ▲ ▲ ▲ ▲

There's a generalization that most men won't ask for directions—no matter what. In fact, may women would say that men won't even admit being lost. Instead, we drive around for hours claiming to know exactly where we are, promising that it will only be another minute until we arrive at our destination, while that minute soon turns into an hour.

Sometimes, for whatever reason, we all feel totally clueless in a given situation. I hate to admit that I didn't know what I was doing when I began my career as a speaker. When I first sent out the video of my presentation, I only wanted confirmation of what I already knew: I was great! Instead, I was offered some constructive criticism to make my speech better. At first, I rejected the comments. My ego was bruised, and people weren't telling me what I wanted to hear. *Obviously, they're jealous or insecure,*

I thought. My overinflated estimation of my talent and ability blinded me, and I was completely unaware of my shortcomings.

But reality has a way of slapping us in the face. I didn't get any bookings from the speakers' showcase, and I had to admit that I was off track. I began to develop a more realistic understanding of my capabilities and was forced to look at myself more objectively. Thanks to the honest assessment and helpful information provided to me, I was able to correct errors early on. Luckily, I asked for directions once I realized I was lost.

I've now noticed that the people who never seem to lose their way call ahead of time to get directions. They ask questions about landmarks, road conditions, the best time to travel, and how much time will be needed. They write the information down and review it along the journey. So when you're embarking on a new adventure in your life, you should do the same. Ask someone who's already traveled in the direction you're going, and listen to his or her directions.

To learn, grow, and excel, you must be open to feedback and instruction. When you're lost or overwhelmed, don't be afraid to say so; by asking for help, you may find the shortest route to success.

CHAPTER 19

CPAE: What Does It Really Mean?

"For I can do anything with the help of Christ who gives me the strength I need."
— Philippians 4:13

E very year, the National Speakers Association presents an award called the "Council of Peers Award for Excellence (CPAE) Speaker Hall of Fame" to no more than five members of the association. It's a high honor, because you must be nominated by another CPAE recipient who bases his or her decision on your material, style, experience, delivery, image, professionalism, and communication.

At the first NSA convention I attended back in 1992, I watched five speakers walk onstage to receive the award and make acceptance speeches, and one thought kept running through my mind: *I'm going to receive the CPAE Hall of Fame award someday.* It became an official goal of mine—I even wrote it down.

Six years later my business was really taking off. I was lecturing at about 194 events per year, which was keeping me extremely busy. But I wanted to be sure that I was still on the right path, so I called one of my mentors, Nido Qubein, to ask him if he'd take a look at my business and give me some counsel on how to make it grow even more.

"I'd be happy to," Nido replied.

I gathered all of my records—including my financial data—and dumped the large pile of paper on his desk. After looking it over, he spent some time with me offering helpful suggestions. Then he leaned over and said, "Keith, your income is in the top 10 percent of all the speakers in the NSA."

I was genuinely surprised—I hadn't stopped to reflect on how far I'd come. I thanked him for his evaluation and went home, thinking, *I'm going to continue to work as hard as I have been in order to stay successful in this business.*

The next year, I was thrilled to learn that Nido had nominated me for the CPAE Hall of Fame award. I was honored, not just to be singled out, but to be endorsed by Nido. He's practically the godfather of the NSA, and he's one of the kindest, most giving, and well-respected men you'll ever meet. Plus, he's been incredibly successful as a speaker—perhaps the most successful in the entire association. On top of it all, he's a humble man of God. So to receive a letter from him saying that he'd nominated me for this honor was an awesome experience.

The time period between being nominated and finding out if you'll receive the award is about four months long. So I had plenty of time to get excited about the possibility of being selected. At the end of my wait, however, I received a letter stating that I hadn't been chosen as a recipient. The chairperson of the committee had attached a handwritten note, saying, "Don't worry. It took me several times before I got it."

I was bummed out. I thought, *It may have taken you several times, but I was nominated by Nido. I'm also having one of the busiest years of any speaker out there, so I should be getting the award this year.* But as I calmed down, I remembered hearing that few people win the first time they're nominated. Most have been in the running for at least three years before actually being voted into the Hall of Fame, and there are those who have been nominated 10 or 12 times and have never made it. So I was grateful that Nido thought enough of me to consider me for the honor.

Nido nominated me again the following year. I thought, *I'll definitely win it this time. I did about 140 speaking engagements, and business was good.* However, four months later, another rejection letter arrived. I was disappointed, but still thankful for the nomination.

The next time was different. Once again, Nido selected me as his nominee, but I also received endorsements from other CPAE award winners. Joe Calloway—a great speaker and a personal friend, mentor, and coach—nominated me; and Rosita Perez, one of the true legends in the speaking business, chose me as well. To my excitement, it wasn't a rejection letter but a letter of acceptance that I received this time around. I was one of the five who would receive the CPAE award at the 2000 NSA Annual Convention, which would be held in Washington, D.C.

I was thrilled, but there was a catch. The rules state that you can't tell anyone your good news until you've been recognized at the convention because the association wants to keep it a secret. The NSA patterns its awards after the Academy Awards®: The audience doesn't know who gets it until the winner is announced the evening of the ceremony. So, for months I had to keep my mouth shut.

The waiting was almost over when I arrived at our nation's capital for the 2000 NSA annual convention. I got there on a

Sunday, just in time to hear my buddy Dan Clark deliver the luncheon keynote address. It was a day full of activity for me: I'd gone to church in the morning, and I'd had conference sessions and a radio interview for my book *Attitude Is Everything* (which had been released a few months earlier) in the afternoon. And not that I ever need an excuse to smile, but my extra-wide grin was tipping people off that I might know something they didn't.

The first person I ran into who sensed that I had a good reason to be cheerful was Willie Jolley, a good friend and a very successful speaker who'd started in the business the same year I did. I was headed toward the elevator when he stopped me midstride.

"Hey, man, how's it going?" he asked.

"Super-fantastic!" I replied enthusiastically.

We exchanged the usual small talk before he asked me, "So what's up? You wouldn't happen to know who's receiving the CPAE Hall of Fame award this year, would you?"

I didn't immediately respond . . . and I hoped that he hadn't noticed my smile getting a bit broader.

"Any chance that *you* might be getting one?" he chuckled.

I looked away for a second, hoping he'd change the subject.

"Man, I'm just joking. But seriously, I strongly believe that one of us is going to win really soon."

"I think so, too," I agreed, and then I made a hasty exit before I gave anything away. *Wouldn't it be great if we both got the award tonight? Now that would be something,* I thought.

I kept running into people I knew, and they all wanted to know why I was grinning like the Cheshire cat. Since my efforts to don a poker face weren't working, I decided it might be best to stay in my suite until the banquet and awards ceremony the following evening. Plus, I wanted to spend as much time as I could rehearsing my acceptance speech.

Standing in front of the mirror with a coat hanger as my microphone, I practiced the words I'd dreamed of delivering for the past eight years. I'd worked hard to be where I was: flying 200,000 miles per year, traveling across the country to share my beliefs about the power of attitude, building a business on sheer determination and faith, sacrificing time with my family and friends, and delaying starting a family of my own. There were many times when I'd wondered if it was all worth it.

But a reflection in the mirror caught my eye. Because of some mix-up with my reservation when I checked in, the hotel had offered me their presidential suite, complete with a grand piano in the corner of the main room. I looked around at my opulent surroundings and realized that I'd made it. I had so much to be thankful for.

I thought back to my first few years in grade school: the teasing and laughter because of my stuttering, all the nights I lay awake and cried because I couldn't talk like the rest of the kids. I remembered my mother telling me that one day I'd stand tall and be able to say my name out loud without stuttering.

While I had no way of knowing it then, my stuttering turned out to be a blessing in disguise. Because of that challenge, I learned to trust in God and to rely on my faith in Him to make a way for me. I'd learned that through discipline, practice, and the love and support of others, the impossible is possible.

Instinctively, I found myself on my knees thanking God for bringing me to this point. I was humbled.

But I was also excited. As I put on my custom-made tuxedo—yes, this was *my* night—I began to regret that I hadn't told anyone, not even my mom, about my receiving the CPAE award. As a rule, I don't make a big deal of my accomplishments; in fact, I have a habit of downplaying a lot of significant events. Yet I know that my family would have loved to have shared this moment with me.

I went downstairs to one of the hotel's huge ballrooms where the dinner and awards ceremony were being held. Some friends of mine, Doug and Gayle Smart, were heading in at the same time and suggested that we grab seats together at one of the tables in the back. That's when I finally let my secret slip: "I'd love to join you, but I have to sit up front." I grinned.

As instructed by Nido during our brief meeting prior to the event, I took a seat at a table that would give me easy access to the stage. I have no idea what was served that night because I was so eager for the program to begin. It had been eight years since my first NSA convention, and I was about to realize the goal I'd been working toward all that time.

The masters of ceremonies, Jim Tunney and Ty Boyd, had both been CPAE award recipients, so it goes without saying that they were very accomplished speakers. Taking their places at the twin lecterns, they brought the festive crowd to order and explained a little bit about the significance of the CPAE Hall of Fame award. Fewer than 150 people have received this award since its establishment in 1977—that's an impressive statistic when you consider that there are currently more than 4,000 members in the NSA.

Naturally, I was on the edge of my seat throughout the introduction. Just when I thought I couldn't wait any longer, Jim introduced the first presenter, Nido Qubein. *Am I going to be the first one announced?* I wondered.

Nido stepped to the lectern and the crowd applauded. Always the epitome of class, he looked stately in his black tuxedo with the bright red pocket square. He smiled and began his speech:

"Ladies and gentlemen: What a pleasure it is for me at this festive gala to introduce our first CPAE Hall of Fame recipient. His life has been a mosaic of generosity and philanthropy; his work has been a tapestry woven with the threads of talent, commitment, and faith; and his platform skills are like a quilt—carefully connected with patches of energy, innovation, and substance. In all that he does and in all that he says, our honoree openly shares his belief in God, his loyalty to his country, his stewardship to his church, and his dedication to his profession.

"He was born in Seattle, where he was an all-star Little League baseball player and an all-American basketball champion. After earning his bachelor's degree in community service from Seattle University, he embarked on a 14-year career with a major Fortune 500 company, where he was recognized as one of its top sales and training executives.

"He has written a bestselling book and enjoyed a meteoric rise in the success of his speaking endeavors—with repeat visits to some of the globe's finest corporations, such as Coca-Cola, Boeing, and Microsoft.

"He's a professional speaker of the highest caliber—his calendar shows it, his fee schedule proves it, and his selection by leading bureaus as a top presenter verifies it. But he still loves going fishing with his dad, and he'll be the first to tell you that he learned much about life from his grandma.

"My dear friends, I'm honored to introduce to you the man who perfected the system for going from novice to pro, the man who focused on transcending success to significance and gracefully went from rags to riches. My fellow NSA colleagues, I'm honored to introduce to you the man Robert Schuller proudly features on his global *Hour of Power,* and *The Wall Street Journal* calls the 'Star with Attitude.' He's by far the tallest friend I have, and I love him so.

"Ladies and gentlemen, the first CPAE for the new millennium: my friend, my brother, Certified Speaking

Professional, Council of Peers Award for Excellence recipient
. . . Keith Harrell."

The crowd burst into applause, which quickly turned into
a standing ovation. As I always do when I approach the stage, I
ran up to receive my award. Nido handed me a beautiful, clear
glass statue of a speaker at a lectern. Meanwhile, Jim Tunney
passed me a microphone. Standing at center stage, I began my
acceptance speech:

"I'd like to give all the praise, all the glory, and all the honor
to my Lord and Savior, Jesus Christ. Through him all things are
possible." The audience burst into spontaneous applause. I
nodded in agreement. We were clapping for the Lord.

"I'd like to thank my family—especially my mom and my
grandmother—for their love, encouragement, and support. I'd
also like to thank Mark Sanborn and the entire CPAE selection
committee. I'm humbled and very honored to receive this award.

"Who would have ever thought that this shy, skinny, tall
kid—a kid who stuttered for most of his life—would grow up to
stand here before you tonight? Only by the grace of God and
through the help and support of others was this possible. Many
of those who gave me a helping hand are in this room tonight—
and you know who you are. Shake the hand of the person on
your left and the person on your right and say, 'He's talking about
me!'" Laughter punctuated the moment as the audience
acknowledged my appreciation. "I *am* talking about you, and I
love you, and I thank God for you.

"I'd also like to thank someone who helped me early on in
my career by inviting me into his office and sharing his entire
marketing system with me. Later, he challenged me to write a
book, he motivated me to start it, and he inspired me to finish
it." Since I knew this gentleman wasn't present at the gala, I
turned and looked directly into the lens of the camera that was

filming the event and said, "Larry Winget, I love you, and I thank God for you."

Once again, applause filled the room.

"I'd like to thank the people who nominated me for this award: Joe Calloway, you're my friend and my mentor. I love you, Joe, and I thank God for you. Rosita Perez, the one and only—I love you, Rosita, and I thank God for your inspiration and support. It truly made a difference.

"And finally, I'd like to thank the person who has made the biggest impact: Nido Qubein." I turned and looked to the side of the stage where Nido was standing. ". . . Nido, please step up here with me." He walked up onto the platform, and I looked straight into the face of my friend.

"Nido, you have made a positive impact on my life—one that will never be erased. You have been so many things: You have been my coach, my mentor, and a role model. You have even been a consultant to my business. But most important . . . ," I was choked up, but I pressed on. ". . . Nido, you've been my *friend.*"

The audience responded with love. I faced them again, regained my composure, and continued.

"Over the years I've come to realize what the three most important moments in life are: the day you're born, the day you become born-again, and the day you discover *why* you were born. I'm here tonight to remind you that you have a purpose. You have been chosen and called to make a difference.

"In one of my favorite books of the Bible, the Book of Proverbs, there's a verse that reads, 'In all of your getting, get understanding.' My understanding of the initials CPAE is <u>C</u>hrist <u>P</u>rovides <u>A</u>ll <u>E</u>xcellence. I give him the praise, glory, and honor. Thank you very much."

As soon as I finished, the room filled with applause that was quickly accompanied by another standing ovation. I walked over to Nido, gave him a hug, had my picture taken with him, and then left the stage and collapsed into my chair with a big smile on my face. Before I could catch my breath, Willie Jolley was at my table grinning back.

"Keith, congratulations! I should have known. I applaud your boldness in publicly acknowledging your faith and giving God the glory."

The festivities continued as the four other honorees—Barbara Sanfilippo, Stephen Arterburn, Michael Aun, and my buddy Art Berg—were inducted into the CPAE Hall of Fame. I got just as much enjoyment from watching them receive their awards as I had in receiving mine. I was proud to be among such a stellar group of professionals, and I saw that there were many worthy people in the audience, too. I knew that I was receiving my reward because of God's grace.

▲ ▲ ▲

LESSON 19:
Christ Provides All Excellence
▲ ▲ ▲ ▲ ▲ ▲ ▲ ▲ ▲

I used to define *excellence* as the ability to do one thing much better than anyone else, even if it meant letting the rest of my life take a backseat. As a basketball player, I was singularly focused on being the best, and I excelled. But the time I put into perfecting my game didn't leave me with much energy for anything else, and as a result, my relationships suffered, my health failed, and I know my grades could have been better. It took being passed over in the NBA draft for me to recognize that things were out of balance, and that excellence means much more than being the best at one pursuit.

My definition for excellence continues to expand. These days, excellence means having spiritual, physical, and financial health, showing sincere love to my family and all those around me, and making an effort to nurture all relationships. Viewed as a measure of perfection, excellence is unattainable. But when it becomes a personal standard for fulfilling lifelong desires and ambitions, excellence is what drives you to become a well-rounded individual leading a healthier, happier, more productive existence. Think about it: What would your life be like if you stopped accepting mediocrity?

Novelist Pearl S. Buck once wrote: "The secret of joy is contained in one word—excellence. To know how to do something well is to enjoy it." I know this is true, because whenever I take the time to do something well, I'm filled with a great sense of pleasure and satisfaction. I believe that we should strive for excellence in every aspect of life and surround ourselves with people who support our growth and who, in turn, we can support. And let us not forget that through God's guidance and grace, we can all achieve excellence—because through Him all things are possible.

CHAPTER 20

In All Your Getting,
Get Understanding

" . . . with all thy getting get understanding."
— Proverbs 4:7

The one driving force in my life is my faith. It's the rock on which I stand, and it's my source of peace. It's everything to me. My spiritual journey has had its highs and its lows, but I know for certain that my Lord and Savior, Jesus Christ, has been with me through everything that's happened during my life.

I've considered myself a Christian for as long as I can remember. My involvement in the church from an early age helped instill certain moral values in me: I knew what was right and what was wrong, and I learned respect for my elders and for authority. But most important, I learned how to have a personal relationship with Jesus.

I went to church on and off from the time I was young. My family attended the First AME Church in Seattle, the church where my mother and grandparents were members. By the time I was 12, I was a member of the Youth Usher Board.

I'd greet people, escort them to their seats, and monitor the door to keep anyone from walking into the sanctuary during certain parts of the service.

One morning after the congregation had taken their seats and the service had begun, I started feeling light-headed. Before I knew what had happened, there was a tremendous *thud . . .* I'd fainted. Everyone scrambled around to see if they could revive me. My mom came over to help, and even the pastor stopped preaching to see if I was okay. It was at that point that my mom decided I didn't have to usher anymore.

As I got older, my mother let me decide whether I'd go to church or not. In high school I stopped attending on a regular basis—except on major holidays, such as Easter Sunday. Although I was a good person, and I always knew when I wasn't keeping the Lord's commandments or conducting myself as a faithful disciple should, I was a lax Christian. I followed the same pattern in college, until I got seriously ill. Like many people who are faced with adversity, when I got sick I went to church more frequently.

Of course, after college I started working for IBM and making fairly good money, which allowed me to drive a nice car and keep up with the latest fashion trends. I was going out, partying, and chasing the girls—all the things I thought I was supposed to do since I was young and single. But there was an emptiness inside of me, and I began to realize that the only solution was to rededicate my life to Christ and have a personal and committed relationship with God.

I still had many questions about God and the way He was working in my life when I read a book called *Releasing Your Potential* by Dr. Myles Munroe. It was one of the first books I'd ever read that addressed serious questions about knowing the role of one's *purpose* in life. Through reading Munroe's book, I discovered that God has a purpose for all of us. It was a real turning point for me, and it led me to ask myself some specific questions, such as: "What is *my* purpose? What am I to accomplish while I'm here on Earth?"

In a wonderful illustration of how God works in our lives, I ended up on a flight to Atlanta with Dr. Munroe just two weeks before I left IBM to start my own business. I had a chance to personally thank him for what his book had taught me. His words on that airplane gave me additional confirmation that I was heading in the right direction:

"Keith, I believe God is going to bless you in your own business. I want you to always remember that God is your source. Continue to stay focused on God so that He can guide and direct you."

When the plane landed in Atlanta, I discovered that Dr. Munroe had an additional two-hour layover there due to a delay, so I was able to spend more time with him. He invited me to an upcoming Christian leadership conference he was holding in the Bahamas. I gratefully accepted his offer and went to the event.

At the conference, top church leaders from around the world spoke on leadership, perseverance, trusting God, and following His plan. I was so inspired by the teachings I heard at those sessions that it led to a time of serious prayer for me, and I left the Bahamas with a clear vision for my business.

God continued to place Christians in my life who were more mature in their faith than I was to provide instruction and support. One such person was my cousin Gina. I was working in Chicago and had made plans to meet her for lunch. As we talked, she said, "Keith, I'm going to a meeting tonight that I think you'd really enjoy."

"What is it?" I asked.

"It's a service led by Dr. Creflo A. Dollar. Do you know who he is?"

"I think I've seen him on TV a couple of times," I replied.

"That's right. He's the pastor of the World Changers Church International in College Park, Georgia. That's pretty close to where you live, isn't it?"

"It's about a 50-minute drive," I answered.

"Anyway, the church started with eight people in an elementary school, and now it has more than 20,000 members," Gina said with excitement. "I think you should come to the meeting—it's at the Rosemont Theater."

"I don't know . . . ," I stalled. I didn't want to commit because I didn't want to let Gina down if I didn't show.

"I'll come all the way from work to pick you up, and we'll go together."

"Tell you what," I compromised. "If I decide to go, I'll just meet you down there, okay?"

Gina agreed, but she had no idea what I was really thinking. The truth was that I had other plans for the evening: I wanted to attend a reception being sponsored by a client. I have to admit that the thought of schmoozing on Lake Michigan was more enticing back then than attending a midweek revival.

After lunch I went back to my hotel room, but God wasn't going to let me just roll over on this one. I found myself having one of those inner conversations: *Why don't you want to go?* I kept asking myself.

Because I'm physically tired, I answered back.

But you're planning on going to the party?

Maybe I won't. Maybe I'll just order room service, watch a movie, and go to bed.

Why don't you take a nap right now? It's only two o'clock. The revival doesn't start until seven. Why don't you see how you feel when you wake up?

I got in bed, fell asleep for three hours, and woke up at five o'clock completely refreshed. I jumped up, took a shower, and dressed to go out . . . not to the party, but to the revival. Before long, I was at the theater's entrance, along with about 5,000 other people!

Hey, I'm one of the lucky ones to be here tonight, I thought, changing my attitude.

Someone ahead of me in line said, "We've driven nine hours to come to hear Pastor Dollar." Some had driven even longer than that.

And I wouldn't even drive 50 minutes to hear him in Atlanta?

I went down to the front row, where Gina said she'd be waiting. But she was nowhere to be found. Then the Holy Spirit took over. "You just get a seat anywhere," the Spirit said to me. "You can sit in the balcony if you want. It doesn't matter where you're sitting because tonight something special is going to happen to you."

Once I sat down, Dr. Dollar walked onstage and started talking about the 66 books in the Bible. He asked the audience a question: "Who wants to profit in life?" All of us raised our hands. "The only way to profit in life is to plant the Word of God. There are 66 books in the Bible; they're 66 bags of seeds. These seeds are the Word of God. If you want to profit, you've got to plant these seeds in your heart and in your life."

Then he went on to speak about tithing. "From Malachi 3:8–10, we learn that if you return to God that which is rightfully His—the first 10 percent—He will open up the floodgates of heaven and pour out a blessing so large you won't be able to receive it all."

That's why God is blessing me, I realized. *I'm not living like a Christian, I'm not going to church, I'm not reading my Bible, but God is blessing me because I tithe 10 percent of my income back to Him.*

I turned to the guy seated next to me. I didn't even know

him, but I asked, "Are you tithing?"

"No, I'm not."

"You've got to do it . . . God just revealed it to me. That's why I've been blessed!"

Several minutes later, the Holy Spirit spoke to me again: "How much more do you think I would do for you, child, if you gave your entire life to Me?" That's when I knew that God wanted me to change my life—to turn away from my worldly living and give myself completely to Him.

So when Dr. Dollar gave an altar call, asking all those who wanted to rededicate their lives to come forward, I jumped to my feet and ran down to the front of the theater. I rededicated my life to Christ then and there, making a total commitment to change my heart, mind, and lifestyle.

When I got back to Atlanta, I made the drive to College Park in order to attend World Changers Church International. As I walked into the World Dome, I noticed the vision for the ministry:

> As we proclaim Jesus, the Christ, as head of the church and the manifested Word of God, our goal is to teach the Word of God with simplicity and understanding so that it may be applied to our everyday lives in a practical and effective manner; thereby being transformed into World Changers—changing our immediate world and all those with whom we come into contact, ultimately making a mark that cannot be erased.

At the end of the service, when Dr. Dollar extended the invitation to join the church, I went forward. I was hungry for the Word. Since becoming a World Changer, I thank God for the ministry because I'm being taught His word with simplicity and understanding. I started going to Wednesday- and

Friday-night Bible Study whenever I was in town.

I remember calling my sister, Toni, to tell her about all that was happening in my life.

"It sounds exciting," she responded.

"It's fantastic," I said. "I've made some important decisions that are going to impact my life and my business."

"Your business?"

I explained all about the principle of tithing, and then I added, "I've decided that I'm not going to speak on Sundays anymore."

"What?"

"Yeah. I'm not even going to speak on Saturdays anymore. I'm going to come home each Friday so that I can attend the Sunday services at World Changers."

Toni was silent on the other end of the phone.

"What's going on?" I asked.

"I'm thinking about your schedule last year," she replied. "Based on what I remember, you had a lot of weekend engagements. Do you have any idea how much money you're going to lose?"

The Holy Spirit gave me the answer to her question: "No, I'm actually going to make *more* money. God is going to bless me because I'll be feeding my spirit. I'm hearing the word of God and growing spiritually, so I know He's going to bless me in all areas of my life."

The following year that's exactly what God did. He blessed me. Even though giving up weekends meant that I was doing fewer speaking engagements, God continued to abundantly provide for me. Now I know that God really wants me to understand the importance of righteousness. After all, it's one of the main messages of the Bible.

How I relate to people now is also centered on the righteousness of God. I can't tear people down and think I'm being righteous, because we're all created in God's image. God is love, and as disciples of Christ, we're to love one another. Discipleship is about love; it's about demonstrating to others God's love for them as well as sharing our love with each other.

In trying to understand the purpose God has for my life, I've come to understand that He has given us all special gifts. I thank God for my gift, which is the ability to communicate. I thank Him for allowing me to deliver my message on attitude—a message that gives hope and motivation. I really believe that the way I live my life and the words that come out of my mouth can have a lasting impact and help make a mark that cannot be erased.

▲ ▲ ▲

I was staying at a hotel one night, and I went over to the fitness room to work out. I met a young woman named Kelly who was in charge of the place. We began a conversation, and before long I was talking to her about attitude, faith, and how God loves her. It was probably one of the best motivational speeches of my life because God used those words to encourage Kelly. Of course at the time, I had no idea that my words were so helpful, but 18 months later, Kelly wrote me a letter of appreciation:

Dear Keith:

Hello! My name is Kelly, and I just wanted thank you for reaching out to me last year. I'm the girl you talked to in the fitness room in February of 2000. (I'd just been diagnosed as severely clinically depressed and was on Prozac.) I wanted to let you know that you motivated me to move to California to pursue my passion for massage therapy. I love to be able to pray for people while I'm doing my massages!

I bought your book, <u>Attitude Is Everything</u>, and loved it! It took me until this year to turn to God completely, but I was fortunate enough to be sent some more wonderful people who have taught me a lot. I want to thank you for the Bible that you sent me; it never leaves my side.

I'm so excited for the plans that God has for me. When I met you, I couldn't understand how you had so much love for God that you made Him number one in your life. Now I get it, and I live my life to serve God with all my heart. Thanks again, and God bless you!

Love,
Kelly

I believe that God wants me to make a positive mark on the lives of other people by getting them to understand the power of having the right attitude. I want people to see just how much God loves them, have faith in His word, and know that He will never forsake them. He keeps His promises.

Trusting God means allowing Him to be the Director of your life. I learned what it means to walk in faith when I left IBM after 14 years, not knowing if I was going to make it in business for myself. I knew I didn't have any customers, nor did I have many prospects. But I also knew that I was going to trust in God: I was being led by Him, and His plan for my life wouldn't allow me to fail.

LESSON 20:
The Spirit Factor
▲ ▲ ▲ ▲ ▲ ▲ ▲ ▲ ▲

My first spiritual advisor in life was my grand-mother. She was a very wise and hardworking woman, who raised her children and grandchildren according to the principles of the Bible. She knew the scripture: "Spare the rod and spoil the child," but she also knew that it was just as important to provide instruction and encouragement.

When I was a young boy, it was my grandmother who taught me right from wrong. She made me understand that there were consequences for my actions and words, to recognize that there was always a right course to follow, and that I should have the conviction and courage to pursue it. As a grown man, when I needed sound advice, I knew I could count on her for counsel. She had the ability to make wise decisions in difficult circumstances, and her good judgment was based on Biblical principles.

In my teen years and during my young adult-hood, I strayed from church, but not from God. I'd been trained in the way I should go, but I got side-tracked in the "me factor" and forgot that it was the "spirit factor" that would fulfill and complete my life.

Nevertheless, at every step of my life and career, God has placed His disciples in my path. They have encouraged, guided, and loved me through the peaks and valleys of life. I've been blessed with many powerful spiritual leaders in my life, too. In my youth it was Pastor (now Bishop) Adams, and later the Reverend Cecil Murray—both powerful men of God in the AME church. And I've been touched and blessed by Dr. Myles Munroe, who took the time to enrich my life one day. Now I'm under the guidance of my pastors, Creflo and Tammi Dollar of World Changers Ministries—my church home.

It's important to me to start each day thanking and praising God and asking Him for guidance. I always thank Him for waking me up and giving me another day. Whatever my need, I take it to God, then I listen for His response. A certain peace comes over me when He answers.

I meditate on certain scriptures and seek guidance. There's an awesome power in prayer, and I know that God moves when we pray. He wants to do more for us than we can ever imagine. I believe that's why the book *The Prayer of Jabez* (by Bruce Wilkinson) is so popular. People are seeking God because they want to experience the fullness of His blessings.

The Holy Spirit is greater than anything outside of us. He helps us grow and become better than we were the day before. His power is there to assist us, to help keep us on the right path of life, give us joy in the midst of trouble, and provide peace in times of trials. The Holy Spirit is the rock on which we stand; He's the source for our peace, comfort, and strength.

CHAPTER 21

Attitude Is Everything

"For as he thinks within himself, so he is."
— Proverbs 23:7

Tuesday, March 2, 1999, the day *The Wall Street Journal* ran the article about me, my phone rang off the hook. I got calls from friends, people I'd lost contact with, people wanting to be speakers and trainers, and a number of literary agents and publicists.

Among the people who called was Jan Miller, one of the top literary agents in the world. She represents people such as Stephen Covey, Les Brown, Tony Robbins, Phil McGraw, and Stedman Graham, just to name a few.

I'd made several attempts over the past two years to talk to Jan about my self-published book, *Attitude Is Everything: A Tune-Up to Enhance Your Life,* but I hadn't been successful in my effort. Now, however, the ball was in my court, and she was trying to convince me that she was the best agent to sell my manuscript and market my book.

"Keith," Jan said over the phone that Tuesday, "you need to

come see me as soon as possible."

"Sure, but I'll be on the road starting on Friday, and I'm not sure when I'll have time to fly to Dallas. I'm booked solid except for Thursday of this week and Friday of next week."

"I guess I'll need to come see *you* then, which, by the way, is something I've never had to do for a potential client. But I'm willing to do it for you. I'll overnight you my press kit and meet with you on Thursday."

I received her package the next day, so by the time she arrived on Thursday, my staff and I were excited to meet her. As soon as she sat down, the conversation began: "So, tell me about *Attitude Is Everything*. And how did you get this article in *The Wall Street Journal?*"

My answer was, "Give God all the glory." Then I went on to say, "Jan, I really don't want to talk about that book. I want to talk about my *new* book, which is going to teach people how to turn attitude into action." I spoke about the ten steps that were going to help people improve the quality of their lives as well as their personal and professional performance.

Jan connected with my vision for the new book. "Let's go to New York. I want you to go with me and sit down with the publishers. I'm going to schedule appointments with all the top publicists, and I want you to tell them exactly what you just told me. When are you available?"

I checked my calendar. "How about a week from tomorrow?"

"Next Friday? Perfect," Jan replied.

I flew into New York the following Thursday night and met Jan the next morning. Starting at 8 A.M., we hit all the main stops, visiting publishers such as Simon & Schuster, Doubleday, and HarperCollins. I did exactly what Jan had told me to do: I gave my short speech about my new book. At that point all I'd written was a single piece of paper with the proposed title and several of the steps I'd mentioned during her initial visit with me.

Five days later, Jan called my office. "Tomorrow we're going to start the opening bid," she said excitedly. I was traveling the following day, but Jan tracked me down on my cell phone. "Great news, Keith—the first bid is big."

I replied, "Give God the glory." It was great news, but I tried to remain calm.

Several hours later Jan called back. "The bid has *doubled* since the opening bid."

"Give God the glory," was all I could say again. I was still doing my best not to get overly excited.

But the next day, Jan called with the closing bid: "Keith, HarperCollins won the bidding. Are you ready for this? We've got it." She was so enthusiastic over the phone. "This is great news! Aren't you excited?"

"Let me ask you a question," I responded.

"Okay."

"Am I going to get the payment in a lump sum or in installments?"

"Usually the contract is paid out in installments. Why do you ask?"

"Because this is going to be the biggest check I've ever been able to return back to the Kingdom of God. It's going to be the largest tithe and offering check I've made at one time . . . *now* I'm excited!"

As I hung up, I started whooping and hollering and running around the room praising and thanking God.

▲ ▲ ▲

Jan was very aggressive in the contract negotiations. She let HarperCollins know that she already had a writer selected to assist me because she knew that they wanted to release the book the first of the year. That put it on the fast track—we had only three to four months to complete the manuscript.

I was really pleased when I met the guy Jan lined up to help me write the book. He came to hear me speak, and I was impressed by his winning attitude. He'd just finished writing a book for a minister, and he was excited about doing one with me.

But for some reason, we got hung up on the contract. One month after I signed my deal with Cliff Street Books/ HarperCollins, we still didn't have a signed contract with the writer—so we were already a month behind. I was getting a little nervous because I knew we had a tight time frame; plus, my speaking schedule was very busy. So, with a good deal of time already behind us, we'd started the formal negotiation process with the writer—only to discover that he had additional demands that he hadn't disclosed when we reached a verbal agreement a month earlier. He wanted more money, his name on the book's cover, and several other perks that we'd said from the start we weren't in agreement with. I guess he felt that he had more leverage with fewer than three months to go, so he was playing his trump card. But with Jan being the super-agent that she is, she held firm to what we had verbally agreed to, and we finally got him to sign a contract.

So the writing began. Since I've always felt comfortable working with a solid core of professionals, I hired Arabella Grayson and Sam Horn, two trusted friends and writers, to assist me in whatever way they could to make sure this book made a difference in people's lives. The good news was that, in the beginning, we all shared the same vision. But the bad news was that a month into the project, the writer took my vision in a different direction, which was problematic for me. From the beginning, he had a vision of how the book should be written. I also had my own ideas. Unbeknownst to either of us, the other key person—our editor, Diane—had a third opinion of how the book should be written. Excuse the pun, but none of us was on the same page.

I think the writer was expecting greater control over the project, and my suspicions were confirmed one day when I received a surprise call from Jan: "He's finished. He quit. He just called to tell me he no longer wants to be on the project."

Being Mr. Attitude, I responded, "Well, it looks like we'll just have to move on without him."

"I've already got another person in mind to do the writing," Jan volunteered.

"No, I think I can pull this off. We're already deep into this project, and I can handle it." I was already thinking of letting Sam be the lead writer and hiring two additional people to assist with the research.

Jan checked with Diane, our editor at HarperCollins. She supported my decision, telling Diane, "Keith is used to building his own teams and making them work. Let's just let him go. He knows the deadline, so let's see if he can do it."

We went another three weeks into the project working on an outline and gathering background material. Finally, I concluded that the deadline was way too aggressive with this many hands in the pot. There were so many different opinions regarding direction, content, flow of material, the audience, and the book's format. Who was our audience? Should it be a self-help book, a spiritual reference work, or should it have a business focus and include exercises? We were running out of time, so I narrowed the team back down to just Sam and me.

We worked hard to put together an outline, but when I

submitted it to Diane, I was in for another wake-up call. We were way off base in terms of where HarperCollins saw the book going, and Sam relinquished her role as lead writer and returned to her own projects.

Jan got back into the mix, and we got on track. We hired another writer, because by now the manuscript was due in a little over six weeks. Wes, the new writer, was not only gifted in his craft, but also had an uncanny ability to type as fast as people could talk. This eliminated the need for tapes and transcriptions, which saved us a huge chunk of time. Remember, all of this writing crunch was coming down in the middle of one of the busiest speaking years I'd ever experienced. *The Wall Street Journal* article had caused my calendar to mushroom, so I found myself talking to Wes from phone booths, cell phones, hotel rooms, limos, and airplanes.

Wes flew in to Atlanta one weekend, and we spent Thursday night through Sunday going through my entire life and talking about the direction Diane wanted the book to take. As I talked, he typed. He took all the information I gave him and went back to work.

Early one morning, before I spoke to a group in Chicago, I received a phone call from Arabella. She wanted to know how the project was going and jokingly asked me whether I still had the same writer. It struck me then that she could really still be an asset to the project since I was spending most of my time crisscrossing the country, and my staff was already overwhelmed with managing my burgeoning schedule.

Initially, I hired Arabella to conduct a series of telephone interviews, transcribe the material, and forward the notes to Wes. It was an interesting process to work with an assistant who lived in California and a writer who lived in Illinois. I'd be calling from all over the country, trying to make myself available, get the necessary materials to them, and check on our progress.

Wes was committed to this project, for which we were all grateful. But I felt that his commitment was starting to become ownership; the book was becoming more his than mine. But we just kept pressing on in order to meet the deadline. I received the first draft of the manuscript *two days* before it was due at HarperCollins. As I read through it, I could see it wasn't the book I had in mind. I made some substantial changes, which I mailed back to Wes. I don't think he was happy with all my corrections, but they were changes I knew had to be made.

Diane received the first draft of the manuscript and was pleased. But we both agreed that there were revisions that needed to be made so that my voice and values were reflected. Arabella and I spent every available opportunity during the next four weeks reshaping and rewriting the book. Pushing myself to near exhaustion, I actually fell asleep midsentence during a few of our marathon work sessions.

At times, my attitude was tested. Since I'm such a perfectionist, any minor grammatical or factual errors often resulted in a verbal lashing from me. I have to admit that I was extremely difficult to work with, but through much prayer we managed to survive frayed nerves, fatigue, and major miscommunication. I thank God for the wonderful people who were committed to me during that challenging time—Joyce Head, who was on my staff then; Carolyn Zatto; and of course, Arabella and Wes.

After three weeks of working around-the-clock, I didn't want to let the manuscript go; I kept making changes and having Arabella send them to Wes. I didn't want to quit until I knew it was just right. Even though this 24/7 schedule was taking a toll on all of us, I pressed on. We had a time line, and my goal was to ensure that the book's content would help change people's lives.

I was on the road speaking the day Wes was due to have the manuscript to HarperCollins. Before my speech, I decided to call Arabella. She'd just received an electronic transmission of the manuscript and noticed right away that some of the passages I'd wanted included were missing, and Wes had retained text that should have been deleted.

"There's more," Arabella added. "It appears that the manuscript was sent to Diane in New York earlier this morning."

As Arabella began reading parts of the manuscript to me over the phone, it became apparent that some of the key elements I'd asked Wes to revise, those regarding my values and vision, weren't accurately reflected. So I called Diane. She was on her way to Europe to interview Pope John Paul II for his upcoming book, and she said she was planning on taking the manuscript with her to read on the plane. "Don't take it with you," I implored. "What you have isn't my complete book. It's missing some important elements. My complete manuscript will be in your hands by the time you return from Europe next week."

"That's less than five days," she replied.

"I can do it."

In just four and a half days, we made all the necessary revisions. It was like studying and taking six final exams in one day, but Arabella and I did it—we made the deadline. It was one of the most difficult endeavors I'd ever embarked upon, but it was also one of the most rewarding.

▲ ▲ ▲

As my team waited for HarperCollins to publish the manuscript, I turned my attention to getting endorsements. I had several people in mind— Lou Holtz, head football coach at the University of South Carolina; Lenny Wilkins, coach of the

NBA's Toronto Raptors; Andy Taylor, president and CEO of Enterprise Rent-A-Car; Stephen R. Covey, author of *The 7 Habits of Highly Effective People;* Stedman Graham, author and entrepreneur; Les Brown, author and motivational speaker; and Tony Robbins, author and life coach. I was able to get all of them, but the best endorsement came from author, motivational speaker, and personal inspiration Zig Ziglar, because even though he didn't know it, we had a history. I'd read his book *See You at the Top* nearly 20 years earlier, and it changed my attitude, which ultimately changed my life. His book made a difference because the word of God was sprinkled throughout each chapter, and the more I read it, the more I believed it. In turn, the more I believed it, the more my actions and my life changed.

James Usher, a colleague who knew Zig personally, had tried to get the endorsement for months, but it seemed that it wasn't going to happen. A couple of weeks had gone by when Juanell Teague called to invite me to a tribute in honor of Zig. He was being recognized for the positive impact his books, tapes, and motivational seminars had made on millions of lives around the world. Naturally, I decided to attend. Call it fate, but a couple of weeks after the event I received a call from one of his assistants, requesting my manuscript for his review. I forwarded a copy to her, and just before the deadline for endorsements she called with some valuable input:

"Zig noticed that throughout the book you referenced the importance of God in your life."

"That's right," I responded.

"You even quote scripture throughout the book."

"True."

"But nowhere in the book do you actually mention that you're a Christian. Why not consider letting your readers know so that there's absolutely no confusion on the issue?"

"You're absolutely right," I said.

"By the way, Zig would be happy to write you an endorsement for your book."

Soon after, I received it.

Exactly one year after *The Wall Street Journal* article appeared, my book, *Attitude Is Everything: 10 Life-Changing Steps to Turning Attitude into Action,* hit bookstores all over the country. It wouldn't have been possible without God, the source of my strength and faith; the relationships I have with my family and friends; or the numerous people who unselfishly gave of their time and talents and shared their wisdom with me. I can look back and see that the primary lessons I've learned are to put God first in my life, follow His commandments, and trust in Him. I thank God for His wisdom and guidance and for teaching me the importance of having an attitude of gratitude.

▲ ▲ ▲

LESSON 21:
An Attitude of Gratitude
▲ ▲ ▲ ▲ ▲ ▲ ▲ ▲ ▲

I'm grateful for the lessons I've learned in life. They've taught me the meaning and value of those things that I hold most dear—my relationship with God, my family, my friends, and all the amazing people I've met along my journey.

I'm most grateful for my relationship with God, for He created me and allowed me to be part of His family. He has blessed me abundantly and given me the greatest gift ever—eternal life.

I'm grateful for my pastor and his wonderful wife. They teach the word of God with simplicity and understanding in a way that allows me to see how to apply Biblical teachings in my daily interactions.

I'm grateful for my family and friends. They've enriched my life in untold ways.

I'm grateful for the loving and caring teachers and coaches who took the time to instruct and nurture me during my formative years. They believed in me before I believed in myself. Without them, who knows what path my life would have taken.

I'm grateful for the mentors and role models who provide me with direction and sound advice. They've shared their strategies for achieving success, transforming and enriching my life.

I'm grateful that I didn't get drafted to play professional basketball. That setback taught me so much: I was hurt and disappointed, and I blamed everybody. To heal, I had to understand forgiveness.

I'm grateful for my experiences at IBM. I got to work for one of the best corporations in the world, and I learned about excellence, professionalism, and the business world. Through the opportunities available to me, I discovered my passion in life.

I'm grateful to God for helping me overcome adversities because through them I've learned some of the greatest lessons of my life—patience, perseverance, faithfulness, courage, and how to hang on to a positive attitude.

I'm grateful for everything. Each day that God gives me is another opportunity to learn and grow.

Each one of us has so much to be grateful for. I thank God for you, and I wish you all the best on your journey toward maintaining an attitude of gratitude.

POSTSCRIPT

● ● ● ● ● ● ● ● ● ● ● ● ●

Had it not been for the motivation and vision of Bill Butterworth, this book would never have been written. I first met Bill when we both spoke at Making a Difference, an annual charity function, in Charlotte, North Carolina. Afterward, we had a pleasant but brief conversation about the industry and were surprised to bump into one another later on in the day at the airport. As we waited in the lounge to board our flights, I began sharing a few of my life experiences: I told him about my relationship with God and how truly thankful I am for the many blessings I've received. Since he's a professional speaker as well as a writer, Bill suggested that I write a book about my life.

I'd recently written *Attitude Is Everything,* so I told Bill I wasn't interested in writing a memoir. Our conversation ended, and I didn't think anything else about his suggestion until he called me at my office in Atlanta a few weeks later to tell me that he'd read *Attitude Is Everything,* yet he felt there was so much more people could gain from hearing my entire story. Bill was convinced that the challenges and turning points I'd faced in my life could give insight to others. He thought that reading about an introvert who overcame stuttering to become a top-ranked motivational speaker might inspire and encourage a few people. I listened, but I still wasn't 100 percent sold.

Bill offered to outline a manuscript based on what he'd read in my book and fax it to me. Thus began our collaboration and the foundation for *An Attitude of Gratitude*. As the process for writing the book progressed, I realized that I needed to do more than simply share my story—I wanted to leave readers with life lessons they could apply to their own experiences.

Through the process of closely examining my own life, I've come to know and appreciate that each of us has a life worthy of examination, lessons to learn, opportunities for growth, and a unique story to share that can be of benefit to others.

If at any point during the reading of this book you asked yourself, "What life lessons do I need to learn in order to grow?" then I have done my job. May you be forever transformed. I wish for you an incredible journey!

ABOUT THE AUTHOR

• • • • • • • • • • • • • • • •

Known across corporate America for his energetic, innovative presentations, **Keith D. Harrell** is a dynamic life coach and motivational speaker. Harrell shares his powerful message, "Attitude Is Everything" with audiences around the world. While growing up in Seattle, Washington, he aspired to become a professional basketball player. Although he never realized that dream, an article in *The Wall Street Journal* referred to him as a "Star with Attitude . . . What sets him apart from less successful speakers is driving ambition, and an attitude that refuses to flag."

As president of Harrell Performance Systems, Harrell has created a firm specializing in helping the corporate marketplace achieve and maintain their goals through the power of a positive attitude. He is a certified speaker, trainer, and consultant and has addressed many of America's top corporations including AT&T, Microsoft, and Kodak. Harrell counts "Big Blue" (IBM) and several other companies such as Coca-Cola among his repeat clients. His signature keynote addresss focuses on ways to meet the challenges of changing technology by understanding the power of human technology.

Harrell earned his bachelor's degree in community service from Seattle University before embarking on a 14-year career with IBM, where he was recognized as one of their top sales and training instructors. In 1997, he received Certified Speaking

Professional designation from the National Speakers Association. In 2000, Harrell was inducted into the CPAE Speaker Hall of Fame, a lifetime award for speaking excellence and professionalism. And one of the country's leading lecture agencies has put him on its list of "22 Guaranteed Standing Ovations."

Harrell is also the author of *Attitude Is Everything: 10 Life-Changing Steps to Turning Attitude into Action,* in which he gives readers a 10-step program for tuning up their attitudes and improving their professional and personal lives. Harrell's Website is: **www.keithharrell.com.**

Hay House Titles of Related Interest

BOOKS

Flex Ability: A Story of Strength and Survival,
by Flex Wheeler, with Cindy Pearlman

Get Out of Your Own Way: Escape from Mind Traps,
by Tom Rusk, M.D.

Inside U: How to Become a Master of Your Own Destiny,
by Grandmaster Byong Yu, Ph.D., with Tom Bleecker

Life Lessons and Reflections, by Montel Williams

*Life's a Journey—Not a Sprint: Navigating Life's Challenges
and Finding a Pathway to Success,* by Jennifer Lewis-Hall

*The Saint, the Surfer, and the CEO: A Remarkable Story
about Living Your Heart's Desires,* by Robin Sharma

CARD DECKS

Comfort Cards, by Max Lucado

If Life Is a Game, These Are the Rules,
by Chérie Carter-Scott, Ph.D.

Power Thought Cards, by Louise L. Hay

The Prayer of Jabez™ Cards, by Dr. Bruce Wilkinson

▲ ▲ ▲

All of the above are available at your local bookstore,
or may be ordered through Hay House, Inc.:
(800) 654-5126 or (760) 431-7695
(800) 650-5115 (fax) or (760) 431-6948 (fax)
www.hayhouse.com

NOTES

NOTES

NOTES

NOTES
• • • • • • • •

NOTES

NOTES

We hope you enjoyed this Hay House book.
If you would like to receive a free catalog featuring additional
Hay House books and products, or if you would like information
about the Hay Foundation, please contact:

Hay House, Inc.
P.O. Box 5100
Carlsbad, CA 92018-5100

(760) 431-7695 or (800) 654-5126
(760) 431-6948 (fax) or (800) 650-5115 (fax)
www.hayhouse.com

Published and distributed in Australia by: Hay House Australia,
Ltd., 18/36 Ralph St., Alexandria NSW 2015
Phone: 612-9669-4299 • *Fax:* 612-9669-4144
www.hayhouse.com.au

Published and Distributed in the United Kingdom by:
Hay House UK, Ltd. • Unit 202, Canalot Studios
222 Kensal Rd., London W10 5BN • *Phone:* 44-20-8962-1230
Fax: 44-20-8962-1239 • www.hayhouse.co.uk

Distributed in Canada by: Raincoast • 9050 Shaughnessy St.,
Vancouver, B.C. V6P 6E5
Phone: (604) 323-7100 • *Fax:* (604) 323-2600

Sign up via the Hay House USA Website to receive the Hay House online
newsletter and stay informed about what's going on with your favorite authors.
You'll receive bimonthly announcements about: Discounts and Offers, Special
Events, Product Highlights, Free Excerpts, Giveaways, and more!